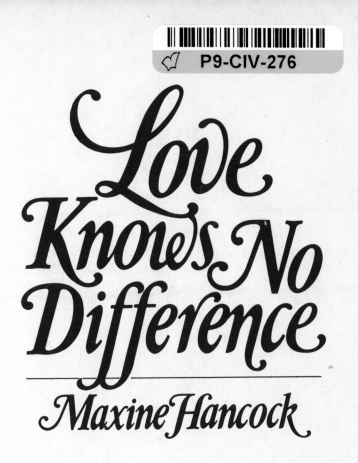

Love Knows No Difference

Maxine Hancock

HARVEST HOUSE PUBLISHERS
Eugene, Oregon 97402

P9-CIV-276

In some anecdotes, names have been altered to protect the privacy of the individuals involved.

LOVE KNOWS NO DIFFERENCE

Copyright © 1983 by Harvest House Publishers
Eugene, Oregon 97402

Library of Congress Catalog Card Number 82-083840
ISBN 0-89081-324-8

Printed in the United States of America.

Dedication

To my friends
at
Bethesda Church, Dewberry,
in the circle of whose love
I have learned much of giving and receiving.

I would learn with you
more of how love gives and receives,
both, with both palms open.
—Luci Shaw

Contents

Introduction

The Season of Giving and Receiving had just passed. The flurry of gift-getting, gift-wrapping, and gift-opening was safely behind us for another year. Yet, as always, the memories that came most quickly to mind are not of *things* but of *people*—not of *gifts,* but of *givers.* The joyful anticipation on a child's face as I begin to open a carefully chosen gift from him; the tranquil relaxation of friends in the lamplit living room; the interchange of laughter and ideas around a big dining-room table—these are the memories of Christmas Just Past.

Partly because this book was on my mind, and partly because I am now forty and more reflective than I once was, and partly because it was the last Christmas to be celebrated with all four of our children still living at home, I was more aware than I had ever been before of the element of grace in the giving and the receiving.

In family and friends, grace surrounds us. Love for family members has very little to do with performance, and a great deal to do with glad acceptance of another. We love each other because we belong to each other. In friendship, the cloak of grace is beautifully reversed, and we belong to each other because we love each other. Friendship is always touched by grace, because it is made from the glad self-giving of one person to another—not for anything that might be gained thereby, but just in the sheer delight of discovery of a person with whom one can share. Each friend is a surprise, a token of grace. And this gift-season was a time for affirming the importance of giving to and receiving from others. How unimportant is the box of chocolates in the hand of a friend! It is the *hand* that is important; that it comes filled with experiences of life to share and outstretched to be filled with our experience; that it knocks at our particular door and not at another.

And so, as I turn my attention to finishing my manuscript, I am moved by the importance of giving and receiving, and

I am aware all over again of how grace flows from giver to receiver, and from receiver to giver.

Once we acknowledge that giving and receiving cannot really be separated from each other, we are on our way to the next discovery: that in love, there is no difference between giving and receiving. In love, it does not matter whether we give or receive. One does not demean us nor the other exalt us. We simply reach out to each other, and find that one hand is for giving and the other for receiving— and that we must constantly be doing both in order to survive as fully human persons.

The idea for this book was originally planted in my mind by publisher Bob Hawkins. He has waited patiently for many months for its fruition. To him, and to his editorial staff at Harvest House, I am grateful. And, of course, I have always those to thank who are closer to home: Bonnie Robinson, who continues to give of herself in the office with a quiet, gracious manner and an expertise I value highly; my loving, supportive family, who make way for me to write.

I gladly acknowledge a special love-debt to a new friend and long-loved poet, Luci Shaw, who personally gave permission for the quotation from "Gifts for My Girl,"[1] which so perfectly states the thesis of this book. That quotation expresses my personal prayer as we enter this book together.

—Maxine Hancock

Part One

~~~~~~~~~~~~~

Giving and Receiving—
Grounded in Grace

~~~~~~~~~~~~~

Freely you have received;
freely give.

1

Freely You Have Received

"Back in those days," the 84-year-old woman reminisces, "we had to help each other. We would never have survived otherwise, you know." She had come from England as a child to be part of the earliest farming community in our area, and her memories are sharp and colorful. "Strangely, though, some of the people who were best at helping others found it very hard to accept help from others. There was one woman in our community like that," she remembers. "She loved to give. Just loved it. If someone were sick, she baked for the family. She was always the first one there to help when someone died or when there were other troubles in a family. But you know, one winter her home was destroyed by fire. And then she offended the whole community by utterly refusing their help. She had loved to offer her help, but she could not bring herself to accept theirs. Pride, you know."

Of course, we have all known—or been—such people. It is, after all, so much easier to give than it is to receive. Yet receiving is an essential of life. The trouble is that, in order to receive, we must acknowledge our need.

I remember with pain and some anger an over-coffee conversation I had several years ago with a younger woman. I had always been a receiver—and a glad one—of second-hand clothes for our children. Each "CARE package," as we called those sprawling clothing boxes which came our way, was received with joy and delight. Opening the box was a sort of mini-Christmas. So it seemed very natural to me to offer to "pass it on," especially since the young woman was complaining to me about the high cost of children's clothing.

"You know," I offered, "I think your daughter would be just the right size for some of the lovely things Heather Ruth has outgrown. In fact, I've been looking for just the right little girl to share them with."

The young woman bridled. "Oh, *really*," she said scornfully. "I may find prices high, but we're not *that* hard up." I felt as though she had slapped my face.

My reply was taut. "That's interesting," I managed. "We've always been that hard up." A strained silence fell across our conversation, the magic circle of giving and receiving broken.

"I hope you're not offended," she offered.

"No," I said, "not offended." But I did not say the rest: not offended, just terribly, incredulously angry at the waste of what should have been a shared joy. No, I was more than angry. I was mad!

But I know that I too have botched the moment of receiving. I have sometimes denied someone else the pleasure of giving or belittled the gift by failing to respond. I am still embarrassed about the old muskrat coat an older friend of mine offered to me. "It's yours," she said, just sort of by-the-way one day. I was nonplussed. If I accepted it, I would have to wear it. If I didn't, I would be rude. I just said nothing at all.

Later, having thought the whole thing over, I decided I could have the coat restyled and truly enjoy it.

"About that fur coat—" I said one day.

"Oh, that." She shrugged. "I've decided to keep it."

In this matter of giving and receiving, we are all learners. Jesus identified the cycle of receiving and giving in the phrase, "Freely you have received, freely give" (Matthew 10:8). Quite simply, if we are ever to be givers, we must first be receivers.

As children, our very survival depends on our being receivers. Our clutching and sucking instincts acknowledge our need of those who provide shelter, support, and sustenance. Why then do we as adults find it so hard to acknowledge our need of other people? Why are we so slow to recognize our interdependence? Perhaps this is just one more area in which we must become like little children again in order to enter into the kingdom of heaven—the kingdom of grace where giving and receiving are all one, and love knows no difference between them.

Let us look at some of the things that stand between us and gracious receiving, recognizing that until we learn to receive, grace-filled giving will be impossible to us.

Pride

"You know," a friend said to me the other day, "after our last Bible study I went home and looked up everything I could about pride—first of all in the dictionary, and it's not very nice at all. Nothing about it is nice. And then I looked it up in a concordance, and there's nothing nice about it in the Bible, either. I had always thought it was something kind of good...but now I know that whatever the Bible means by pride, it is something I don't want."

She spoke for all of us. Our culture teaches us that pride is a good thing, a fine thing. Sadly, we confuse *pride*—an arrogant, ugly, overweening thing which many theologians see as the root of the original sin—with *self-esteem*—a necessary element of healthy living. When respect for myself as an individual outgrows its proper bounds, it pits me against God and against my neighbor. And so, the Scripture says, "God opposes the proud" (James 4:6). Pride is the wedge that drives itself between giver and receiver in an ugly separation of person from person, of need from gift.

To receive is to acknowledge need. "Ask, and it will be given" (Matthew 7:7) is Jesus' formulation, since what God desires to give us cannot be received until we are ready to ask. To ask is to acknowledge our need. In the Book of Revelation, speaking through John to the church, Jesus Christ speaks in unmistakable anger to a church that refuses to ask:

> You say, "I am rich; I have acquired wealth and do not need a thing." But you do not realize that you are wretched, pitiful, poor, blind and naked (Revelation 3:17).

It is pride which keeps us from God. Salvation is the free gift of God granted to those who ask for it; therefore, those who cannot bring themselves to acknowledge need cannot experience grace.

And it is pride which keeps us from each other. I have often wondered why it is so hard to ask for prayer for our own needs. Is it because our hearts know the truth that "the lesser person is blessed by the greater" (Hebrews 7:7), and hence we resist the blessing of having others lift us and our needs in prayer?

I remember how hard it was, one warm summer day, to get out of my car and walk into my friend Lucetta's bookstore. I dropped in there often, sharing a natural bond of interest with another book-person. But that day I was going to her with a request. I was going to ask her to pray for me.

I had struggled against the Inner Voice that had been insisting that day, "Go and ask Lucetta to pray for you." Everything in me was protesting. I ministered to others. I was the one to whom others came for prayer and counsel. And now I had to go to my friend with an acknowledged need.

Why should it be so hard? The need was clear enough. An allergy to tobacco smoke had become so acute that I was finding it increasingly difficult to live normally let alone to travel as a writer and speaker. Whether eating in restaurants or shopping on a mall, normal outings left me enervated and congested. Social outings were out.

Of course I had prayed about it. I had screwed up my face and my faith and had prayed positively: "Lord, heal me now." The Lord had not seemed the least bit impressed. When that didn't produce results, I had begged God to set me free to live, to be with people. And now I had the strong sense that this little bookstore was the place I was to be, that it was here that I was to acknowledge my need.[1]

Lucetta and I exchanged a few words of greeting, and then I burst into tears. "I came to ask you to pray for me," I blurted, miserably enough. It was one of the shortest—and hardest—sentences I had said in a long while. Together we walked to the store-room at the back of her store. There, surrounded by crates of books and sitting on others, we prayed. Lucetta laid her hand on my shoulder and prayed for me. And then she said quietly, "I believe that God will heal you, Maxine, gradually, through the 'renewing of your mind.' "

The Lord did heal me, just as Lucetta had said, through the "renewing of my mind" (Romans 12:2). He taught me first how to obey Him by bringing stress factors in my life into balance with my physical capability; He taught me how to say "no" more often. Then He showed me—and set me free from—the reaction of fear which had become part of my response to exposure to allergens. Gently He set me free from the narrow little box I had come to live in, and restored me to health—but I was a different person when He was finished healing me. At last I was able to live comfortably and obediently within my own limitations. Through my illness God had tucked me into my own home, where He could teach me a thing or two. He had taught me to accept the physical makeup He had given me. And He had also taught me my need of the ministry of other people in the Body of Christ. I had asked, and I had received.

False Sense of Independence

Repeatedly in the Old Testament, God's people are warned about the dangerous effects of affluence. "When you eat and are satisfied, be careful that you do not forget the Lord" (Deuteronomy 6:11,12). Affluence to some degree or another is the lot of most of us in North America. It is particularly dangerous because it breeds that false sense of independence in which we pay only lip service to our dependence on God, and simply fail to recognize at all our dependence upon other people.

In economic hard times, people notice the phenomenon of people helping each other, of cooperation for survival. A friend of ours who escaped from Hungary after the Revolution of 1957 is highly indignant about the trend in our society toward treating survival as an individualistic, aggressive skill. He talked with me one day, angered by a radio program in which survival training had been described as a series of lessons in how to grab food from other people and in general how to look out for Number One. "They don't know what they're talking about," he told me. "That's not what survival is all about. Human survival is achieved by cooperation and mutual assistance, not by grabbing and clawing. I saw it in Europe during World War Two and in Hungary during those days in the 1950s. People survive by caring for each other—not by this animalistic nonsense."

I can only hope that we will rediscover our interdependence. Perhaps, as lifestyles become more stringent and we reevaluate the meaning of discipleship and service, we will find our way back to each other's doors, carrying our clean, empty cups in acknowledgment of our need of each other.

Even though affluence has cushioned our interactions and given us a false sense of independence, the true state of human interaction is that of interdependence.

I remember being upset when an editor changed one word

in an article of mine and utterly altered my meaning. Now please understand: I love editors, and most of them have to change more than one word in polishing my material for publication. I used to protest, but now I recognize their expertise and gladly accept their help. But in this particular case the one-word change really ruined by article. I had written about our chosen lifestyle of mutual serving through job-sharing and had said, "Cam and I are determined to find ways to express ourselves as two fully *interdependent* persons." The printed article reads, "...as two fully *independent* persons." That is just what I *didn't* want to say! I need Cam. He needs me. We are mutual receivers, "heirs [together] of the gracious gift of life" (1 Peter 3:7).

What is true within marriage is also true in all relationships: any relationship which becomes more than mere acquaintance is based on giving to and receiving from one another. Within those special bonds of love which Christians experience in the church, this interdependence must be continuously acknowledged as we receive from other people and then find opportunity to give in return in what I have heard described as "the mutuality of ministry."

We need God. We need each other. It is this which we must acknowledge. Whatever makes us feel we can go it alone, without God or without each other, is a delusion, a false impression of independence. Only as we acknowledge our interdependence can we learn how to receive.

Misunderstanding Grace

The third impediment to learning how to receive is our limited understanding of grace. We may know, of course, that "by grace [we] have been saved, through faith...it is the gift of God" (Ephesians 2:8). But we don't really come to terms with the fact that receiving God's special grace should make us more open than ever before to the common grace that is all around us—grace that comes to us through nature and through other people. And because we narrow the operation of God's grace to that which is specifically "spiritual," we live impoverished lives when we could be rich if we would simply stretch out our empty hands to others.

Grace sets us free to receive as well as to give when we realize that it is meant to encompass our whole life. Grace sets us free to be both receivers and givers, for it quite literally turns the world upside down for us. All of the old adages ring false: "You don't get something for nothing" is just not true in the kingdom of God. "You get what you work for" is equally false. "Gimme never gets," that old schoolyard taunt, is antithetical to the spirit of the gospel, which teaches us to cry out in our need and freely receive.

Receiving operates in an entirely different spirit from getting. *Getting* is clutching and grasping, indifferent to the source of the good we seek. *Receiving* acknowledges that every good thing has its source in God. It recognizes that He mediates that good through people and processes and circumstances. Receiving means being gratefully aware both of the Source of all good and of the channels through which that goodness comes into our lives. Whether it be the goodness of love through family and parents, the goodness of companionship through friends, the goodness of prayer through the church, the goodness of wisdom through teachers and those who have lived long and well, "every good and perfect gift is from above" (James 1:17).

The spirit of receiving is also very different from the all-too-familiar attitude of demanding. Demanding is selfish, basically at odds with concern for the good of others, whether individually or in society as a whole. Receiving does not demand, but accepts with great joy the good things that are granted by grace. It "makes its requests known" and then enters into peace, resting in God's goodness. This is little understood today, when faith is often confused with presumption. True prayer is the acknowledgment of the privilege of fellowship that is ours through grace. We are invited to voice our requests, to acknowledge our needs. But we have no right to make demands.

I learned something about this when one of our children was about a year old. Sitting in his high chair, he banged and rattled his tray in angry impatience as I prepared supper. In exasperation I turned to him and said, "Can't you see that I'm getting you something good? Can't you just wait quietly?" And even as I spoke to the child, God spoke to me. I suddenly realized that my prayers were very much like the baby's demands: impatient, oft-repeated, demanding. It was time for me to do some growing up myself, to realize that God's plans and purposes were "something good," and that prayer was at least as much an expression of quiet trust as of making my requests known.

Just the other day another little child showed me once more the trusting attitude of receiving. The church family was gathered at our home for a Snow-Fun evening. I was busy in the kitchen when a four-year-old, brushing the long strands of blonde hair out of her eyes, asked very quietly, "May I have a drink?"

I was just filling the coffee urn from the tap, so I put her request on hold. The little girl disappeared—and when next I saw her, maybe half an hour later, her cheeks were rosy. She had been out skating. Her voice was still sweet and gentle. "Now may I have a drink?" she asked. She had a glass of cold water in an instant, and I felt the desire in my heart to be such an asker, such a receiver.

Freely Receive

We receive freely when we recognize that we cannot earn the right to life—or to anything good within it—any more than we can earn the right to God's favor. It is all grace, and comes to us out of God's impartial, free-flowing providence—something the psalmist wondered at again and again in an oft-repeated chorus of praise to "God's steadfast love."

We receive freely when we receive without clutching the gift to ourselves and calling it "mine." Receiving freely means holding God's gifts in an open hand so that we could, if necessary, say with Job, "the Lord gave, and the Lord has taken away; may the name of the Lord be praised" (Job 1:21).

We receive freely when we are able to receive without notions of "paying back." Some people cannot bear to be "obliged," as the old term has it. And so, the instant they have received a favor or a gift, they feel duty-bound to return one. Since giving, like all other good things in our world, has been scarred by selfishness, we do sometimes encounter gifts with implied obligation. The business community used the phrase "He owes me one," with favors treated as tradable commodities. But the person who receives freely accepts a gift as a moment of grace, and perceives in it no obligation other than gratitude to the giver and the continuation of the cycle by passing on a kindness to someone else.

The other day a guest was returning from our home to Edmonton to catch a plane. We wanted to have someone meet her at the bus depot and take her to where she was staying for the night. I found myself thinking about friends and family in the city, and asking myself, "Is there anyone who owes us a favor?" The thought actually made me laugh. I had the sudden glad liberty of knowing that, while we had many friends in the city, we had none who was the tiniest bit obligated to us. Instead, we called one of those dear, free friends and frankly acknowledged our need. "Could you help us?"

What joy, then, in the hearty response, "Why, of course! What can we do to help?"

That is the freedom of receiving by grace, of owing nothing but love, and of having no claim but need. Accepting the help and gifts and person of others becomes as natural as accepting the life-supporting air we breathe—and as necessary. Freely we have received...freely give.

2

Freely Give

When it was first given to me, I quite enjoyed it: an attractive table center made of a perfectly shaped miniature loaf of bread, surrounded by biscuits and pine cones, all sprayed with shellac. But as the days went on, and I moved the decoration from the center of the dining table to the coffee table, then onto a nearby shelf, I began to feel uneasy about that little varnished loaf. True bread though it was, it just sat and gathered dust. It was carefully preserved, lovely to look at—and utterly useless. There was only one thing, finally, to do with it.

But before I reluctantly threw it out, the varnished loaf had shown me something very important: the danger of "secondary purposes," of being attractive and admired while missing the very purpose for which we are created. Bread, after all, is made to be broken, to be eaten, to be shared. And as I looked at that perfect little loaf for the last time, I prayed, "Please, Lord, don't let me be a varnished loaf.

Let me be bread broken, given to the needs around me."

To give freely, to be bread broken to the needs of those around us—that is our calling as disciples of the One who called Himself "the Bread of Life." But that kind of availability does not come easily for most of us.

We have examined some of the attitudes that make it hard for us to receive the grace-filled gifts of life that surround us. Now let us take a look at some of the things that make it hard for us to give as we ought to—freely, joyfully, gratefully.

Possessiveness

Some people seem to just naturally have more "give" in them than others. Some people seem to be born givers. Not I. I am a haver and holder. I like to be able to say "mine" and really mean it. The trait showed up early. A picture in our family album shows me at two, my feet barely projecting over the edge of a child's wicker rocker, holding tightly a blanketed bundle containing my newborn sister. The picture is captioned with my words: "Margie mine."

Since Marg turned out to have a strong, independent streak and early made it clear that she really was not mine at all, I transferred my possessiveness to things that could not talk back—such as my pet frogs, loved and cared for, and, when they died, buried with due attention to detail. And later, there were books—quickly and permanently claimed by the inscription of my name.

Of course, this possessive tendency shows up in other places too. "My children," I say proudly, and then, blushing, mumble a correction: "Our children." And so, when I set out to write a book about a lifestyle characterized by giving, I am writing as a learner. I have been learning, slowly and often painfully, to uncurl my fingers from around the things I love, to be a giver as well as a receiver.

While some people may be more naturally generous than others, I think that most of us learn the word "my" and "mine" very early, and never really unlearn them. Allowing what is "mine" to become "yours" is the essence of giving—its painful essence.

A paradox exists in this matter of owning and giving. Without some sense of ownership, no gift can be given, for I may give only that which I own. As Marcel Mauss points out in his study *The Gift* (New York: Norton, 1967), no society develops gift-giving rituals until a system of ownership has been established.

But while in societal terms I must own something before I can give it, the idea of possessing in any ultimate way is in fact a delusion. Screwtape writes to his understudy devil, Wormwood:

> The sense of ownership in general is always to be encouraged. The humans are always putting up claims to ownership which sound equally funny in Heaven and in Hell, and we must keep them doing so.... And all the time the joke is that the word "Mine" in its fully possessive sense cannot be uttered by human beings about anything. In the long run either Our Father or the Enemy will say "Mine" of each thing that exists....[1]

Something in our fallen hearts claims ownership "in its fully possessive sense" of everything from things to people—ownership that is at best temporary, and, in the case of people, impossible. In the face of our few brief years on this planet, what can ownership really mean? Cam and I "own" a farm. At least we think we do! ("You think that you own a farm, Willie," says the carefree Tam in Carol Ryrie Brink's *Lad With a Whistle*, "but indeed 'tis the farm which owns you.")[2]   One day, as I was driving down a graveled country road lying between farm fields, I tried to think about what the word "own" really means. It means that we get to make payments on the land. It means that we are responsible for the taxes. It means that we can grow crops and make management decisions about that land. It means that we will give account to God for our use or abuse of the good earth. But a person whose lifespan is at best 80 little years, and who probably can "own" the land for only 40 years of those, can hardly be said to "own" land that has been aeons of years in the making.

All that "owning" land can really mean is this: what happens to that piece of property will affect us. If an oil company decides to drill on it, the decision affects us. If the county reassesses it, and raises the taxes, we will be affected. If a government should decide to expropriate it, we would be affected by that decision. One has only to reflect on the fate of the *kulaks*—those sturdy Russian landowners who were shipped wholesale to Siberia during collectivization—in order to imagine the grim possibilities of what "owning" might mean.[3]   But while any of these things would affect us, we are helpless to make or alter these determinations. Our "ownership" merely links us to the land.

A.W. Tozer writes memorably about "The Blessedness of Possessing Nothing":

> The way to deeper knowledge of God is through the lonely valleys of soul poverty and abnegation of all things. The blessed ones who possess the Kingdom are they who repudiated every external thing and have rooted from their hearts all sense of possessing. These are the "poor in spirit"...these blessed poor are no longer slaves to the tyranny of things...though free from all sense of possessing, they yet possess all things. "Theirs is the kingdom of heaven."[4]

It is actually in the freedom from clinging, from holding on to what we "own," that we are set free to give. Paul describes the paradox this way: "...poor, yet making many rich; having nothing, and yet possessing everything" (2 Corinthians 6:10). As those who have given all to God, all that is in our hands is His. We are called merely to be His administrators. "Each one should use whatever gift he has received to serve others, faithfully administering God's grace in various forms" (1 Peter 4:10).

Selfishness

We are born selfish. Parents who have closely observed their infants are aware of this fact. Infants demonstrate, in its raw and most demanding form, the nature of human selfishness. Of course, some of this is a built-in survival kit. But as the child begins to express himself, the parents soon discover that the child demands attention beyond the meeting of needs—beyond that which even the most devoted parent is able to give. And when a second child joins the family, or a neighbor child comes to play, the possessive, jealous nature of a toddler is often surprisingly passionate.

The process of socialization supresses this selfishness and teaches it acceptable ways of expression. By the time we are adults, we take considerable pains to conceal the rawer evidences of our selfishness. But it is nevertheless there—hidden, to be sure—but still a central, driving force.

In recent decades, society has become more tolerant of basic human selfishness. Contemporary thought sees selfishness as necessary to the evolutionary development of the human race. This perception hastens us toward a society ruled by the law of the jungle—"Life is for the strong." But no matter how we intellectualize it, selfishness is still a demanding god. Selfishness opens a maw of personal demand for gratification into which all of life can be fed with nothing left to show for our having lived.

This worship of the god of Self emanates from our central core of selfishness. It is one of the idolatries which is set aside when a person invites Jesus Christ to be Lord of his life. This does not mean that a new Christian is instantly unselfish in all areas. What it does mean is that the Holy Spirit begins to show that person the ugliness of self-worship, along with the falseness of the worship of things which cannot even be possessed. The release into giving begins from the moment of commitment.

For some people there may be an instant release. That was the experience of a friend of ours. He had been a minister for nearly 20 years before he personally experienced the grace of God. It happened that he was at a meeting one night where the speaker said, "If you are not sure that you have received new life in Jesus Christ, why not just step forward now." To our friend, this was radical. Altar calls were not within his liturgical framework. But a hunger in his heart urged him to go, and he did. Kneeling at the front of the church, he invited Jesus Christ to come into his life.

"I didn't feel a lot of emotion," he says, "but on the way home something happened that confirmed that I was indeed a new person in Christ. We stopped for coffee, and as my friends and I rose to leave the table, I did something that was for me totally uncharacteristic, totally new. I had always been know to be 'tight.' My friends knew all too well my ability to outfumble everyone when it came to paying for anything. But that night I reached for the bill. Suddenly I *wanted* to pay. I had been set free to give!"

Not everyone can testify to such a sudden, glad release into giving. For some people it seems a long, slow process by which God converts the soul. But it is begun at the moment of the personal "Yes" to the Lordship of Jesus Christ. On days when I feel most discouraged and still half-pagan, I remember that "he who began a good work in [me] will carry it on to completion until the day of Jesus Christ" (Philippians 1:6). And so I pray: "Don't abandon me to my destructive selfishness, my clutching possessiveness, my Lord. Keep teaching me until all is truly released to You."

Fear

Another enemy of giving is fear. Behind much of our holding onto things is a basic attitude of mistrust. We hang onto what we have because we are afraid that it cannot—or will not—be replaced. And in that attitude we continuously affront our Maker, who taught us to pray simply, "Give us each day our daily bread" (Luke 11:3). The picture behind that prayer is that of the daily supply of manna in the wilderness. The Israelites were to gather enough for just one day. To gather more, to try to carry it over to the next day, was to doubt the dailiness of God's provision.

In our security-consciousness we cling to what never can be made secure. "Do not wear yourself out to get rich," runs an ancient Hebrew proverb. "Cast but a glance at riches, and they are gone; they...fly off to the sky like an eagle" (Proverbs 23:4,5).

But we not only fear for our financial security and therefore give of our material resources reluctantly. Another kind of fear blocks the even more important kind of giving—the giving of ourselves to others. That is the fear of rejection. There is nothing more terrifying than offering a gift while sensing the possibility of its rejection.

I remember the day I delivered some eggs to an estranged friend. All the way to her house I tried to convince myself that I should just turn around and go home. Just because a woman had left the eggs with me didn't mean I had to deliver them. Surely I could just call and tell her to pick them up. But the urgency was there—go, offer, take the risk. I stood at her door and rang the bell, the flat of eggs balanced rather precariously as dogs and cats tumbled around my feet. It seemed an eternity before she answered, and her first expression was less than welcoming. But somehow she accepted both the eggs and myself. Our friendship was restored.

There is no way to gainsay that giving implies risk. Of course it does. But so does living. So does loving. So does anything really worthwhile in human existence. The fear of rejection, actually an inverted form of pride, has to be set aside if a person is to enter into the joy of giving with the glad abandon of one who is accepted by God and can therefore risk the rejection of all other people.

To hold back from giving because of fear of loss of security—or of face—is highly ironic. I think that one of the points Jesus makes in His story of the shrewd manager is that it is the person who has given to others who has built the best security for himself (Luke 16:1-13). And He warned us in the Sermon on the Mount against laying up treasures where "moth and rust destroy" (Matthew 6:19). I do not think He was suggesting that we should be improvident regarding the future. But we do need to remind ourselves that we often lose what we hang onto, while what we give becomes both a temporal and an eternal investment, with rewards both in this life and the next. "One man gives freely, yet gains even more; another withholds unduly, but comes to poverty" (Proverbs 11:24).

To all of these problems which stand in the way of our becoming givers, our Lord Jesus Christ answers from the cross. Not long ago I received a note from fellow author Ron Klug in which he said, "One of my favorite pieces of art is Matthias Grunewald's Isenheim altarpiece...." I followed his lead and looked up a book containing reproductions from that work: the tortured, truly human, truly dying Christ. As I meditated on the death of our Lord, led to reflection by the cruelly twisted hands and feet and pain-distorted face of Grunewald's gray-skinned Christ, I realized in a new way how that ultimate giving addresses all of the problems which would keep us from being givers.

In answer to the problem of selfishness, Our Lord invites us to die to the claims of ourselves and live daily for God. He literally invites us to share in His dying, share in His cross (Matthew 16:24-26).

In answer to the problem of fear and insecurity, we can cry with Paul, "He who did not spare his own Son, but gave him up for us all—how will he not also, along with him, graciously give us all things?" (Romans 8:32).

In answer to the problem of our fear of rejection, we find One who was "despised and rejected by men" (Isaiah 53:3) hanging before our view, offering His love and acceptance to each of us.

"Thanks be to God for his indescribable gift!" (2 Corinthians 9:15) is our awe-filled whisper at the cross. And then, so gifted, so graced, we turn to become givers ourselves.

Part Two

The Gifts We Share

What can we give? What receive?
Here are some gifts that have no price tag,
a catalog for those who are willing to give
no less than themselves.

3

The Gift of Laughter

I grew up surrounded by laughter. Some of the laughter was provided, consciously or otherwise, by guests who stayed with us. Missionaries we found to be the best and funniest. They knew the greatest stories and could laugh at themselves—or at us—most resoundingly. Then there were the preachers. Some of them were fun and funny, and some were not. But even the stuffy preachers provided us with laughter. We did wonderful takeoffs on their serious piety after they left.

But there was one person who stayed in our home with whom we dared not laugh. She had experienced, as a teenager, one of the great revivals. That had been years ago, but she was still doing overflow or afterglow speaking. She was a plain, dour woman, no doubt incredibly sanctified, but without even a glimmer of humor in her. I remember deciding firmly that if revival produced somebody that cold, someone from whom the joy of life had been that thoroughly squeezed, I could get along without it.

I have known only a few sour Christians. In fact, I am irritated by preachers who chide about long faces. I know people with cute little round chubby faces who aren't all that in love with life. It is too bad, however, that people outside the church have seen so many negative Christians that they have become the stereotype of churchgoing believers—you know, the ones like Mrs. Bogart in Sinclair Lewis's *Main Street*: "soft, damp, fat, sighing, indigestive, clinging, melancholy, depressingly hopeful."[1] But while I have known some dyspeptic Christians like that, I have lived among many happy ones, ones to whom laughter is a natural and a holy grace, a complement to every family meal and the glad response to God's goodness.

Laughter—freeing, liberating laughter, freely offered and freely joined in—is a natural response to grace. The fact that such awkward, graceless creatures as we should be the special objects of God's love should surely cause everything from a low, irrepressible chuckle to an outright guffaw. The psalmist says, "The Lord takes delight in his people" (Psalm 149:4), and I have on occasion wondered if some of that pleasure was not a roar of happy laughter.

Laughing With God

It was at a young people's meeting (back when the earth was cooling, my teens remind me), that I accompanied a soloist singing "My God and I." I remember struggling with both the score and the lyrics—words which faintly shocked my very proper mind: "We walk and talk as good friends should and do / We clasp our hands, our voices ring with laughter."[2]

But since then I have learned that fellowship with God does indeed include laughter, a gift He gives us to share with Him.

I shared the gift of laughter in prayer one day with Marguerite. She had told me a long and harrowing story of the way in which the Hound of Heaven had followed her down the "labyrinthine ways" of her life. At last I asked her if she wanted to invite the Lord Jesus Christ, her faithful Pursuer, to come into her life. She realized that the time had come.

I waited while she sought words, waited while she tested and discarded a number of beginnings for her prayer. I waited, praying silently that grace and faith would be given her for this, the most difficult of all of life's turnings. Finally she blurted out, "Dear Lord, I guess You always knew You'd get me in the end." And then we laughed. It was laughter that shared in the rejoicing of the angels around the throne, rising in tiers, layer after layer.

And as we laughed together, there was healing and release from struggle. She entered into the joy of capitulation to the divine Conqueror. Glory and grace washed over us. It was a high and holy—and hilarious—moment.

Irreverent? I do not think so. I have come to hear, and bit by bit to echo, the laughter of God in so many details of our lives. I think I heard His chuckle when, soon after my first book was published, my publisher invited Cam and me to be guests at the annual Christian Booksellers Association convention. "It'll be in Anaheim this year," the sales manager said, and it seemed as though I could hear a brass band playing in the distance. "We'd like for you and Cam to be our guests."

With all the savoir faire of a farmbound wife who had lived for the previous ten years right off the map, I asked the obvious question: "Where's Anaheim?"

Well, the sales manager located it for me: geographically, near Los Angeles. Experientially, the home of Disneyland.

Still picking ourselves up and dusting ourselves off from the business crash which I tell about in *Living on Less and Liking It More*, we were so poor that we weren't sure if we could afford clothes for the trip. We flattened our already-slender savings account to get a suit for Cam; a friend sewed for me. Then, with free Disneyland tickets tucked in our pockets by a friend who had some left over from his recent visit there, we set out for an amazing, all-expenses-paid trip. Our laughter of sheer incredulity met and mingled with the kindly laughter of a loving God.

Yes, I am sure that God laughs. The psalmist pictures Him

laughing derisively at attempts to dethrone Him, laughing at puny man's efforts to seize and usurp His rule.

But I think He has other tones of laughter too—laughter heard only by those who are part of His family, those who gather around His table and really come to know Him.

Laughing With Others

Some people have the unique gift of making others laugh. Others share in the joy by receiving and responding to that gift. Of course, the ability to hold up a comic mirror to life is a commercially salable commodity. But it is not the laughter from the platform nor the canned laughter on the tube, but the laughter in everyday life that is the greatest treasure.

I married Cam for his sense of humor. And it has turned out to be a very good reason. For us, wedding bells were an introduction to peals of laughter. And now, with witty teenagers sparring with us and with each other across our supper table, the laughter is multiplied and amplified.

There was, for instance, the time that Heather Ruth was setting her glass back down. It crashed noisily against her plate and, anticipating our displeasure, Heather swiftly raised the glass high in the air and proposed, "To the Queen."

Now, of course, not everyone thinks that fast. I know I don't. But all can share in the gift of laughter—giving or receiving being equally important to the shared moment of delight. Really, the key to enjoying laughter is a healthy de-escalation of one's own sense of importance. To be sure, personal worth is a good thing and something to be valued. Personal *importance* is quite another matter. It sets us on the road to pomposity. The success of most great comedians is that, in allowing us to laugh at them, they invite us to laugh at ourselves. This laughter deflates our little balloons of personal self-importance. Like Winnie the Pooh after Christopher Robin pops his honey-finding balloon, we find ourselves suddenly back to earth, full of gorse-thorns, but ever so much more livable.

Our age is one which is much too serious about itself. It is deadly serious, for instance, about the pursuit of happiness. It's grim business, this happiness we're supposed to get out of life. We spend a lot of time analyzing and introspecting, and then we discover that happiness, like a fragile butterfly, has eluded our heavy-handed attempts to catch it—and all we have is a little gold dust on our clumsy, grasping fingers.

It is an age which is far too serious about sex, too. In a strangely ironic way, while sex in all its forms and perversions is the base for much of the debased humor in our entertainment media, it is at the same time very serious business. Manual in hand, couples practice coupling, attempting to perfect technique. Balderdash! Bedrooms, as well as kitchens and living rooms, should be places for laughter. I realize that this does not sound very black-sheer and lacy. But I think it is healthy and freeing. And it gets us away from seeing sex as performance.

"We young women have our own hang-ups," one young wife said at a marriage conference. "In fact, hang-ups with kinks in them. We keep wondering, 'How am I doing?' " Laughter liberates; it says, "We're doing fine, however we're doing!" It de-escalates sex and makes it a normal, happy, and holy part of human life.

Although laughter is a true friend to grace, we even have a tendency to be too serious about our own piety. I don't think we can ever be too serious about ultimate things: knowing and pleasing God is a solemn thing, and failing to do so is unspeakably serious. But do we have to be so pompous about our particular way of going about it? I am glad for the gift of satire. I encountered it first, with a sharp intake of breath, in *His* magazine as a university student. Later I would chuckle over *The Wittenburg Door* as it lampooned my treasured cultural forms of religious expression.

Annie Dillard, writing in *Holy the Firm* about her experience in a small church, says:

> The higher Christian churches...come at God with an unwarranted air of professionalism...as though they knew what they were doing, as though people in themselves were an appropriate set of creatures to have dealings with God.... In the high churches they saunter through the liturgy like Mohawks along a strand of scaffolding who have long since forgotten their danger. If God were to blast such a service to bits, the congregation would be, I believe, genuinely shocked. But in the low churches you expect it any minute. This is the beginning of wisdom.[3]

As a "low churcher," I chuckle and await the blast.

Holy and Unholy Laughter

Like all the other good gifts of life, laughter can be overdone or debased. The Scriptures tell us that "fools mock at making amends for sin" (Proverbs 14:9), and that is surely unholy laughter. Another line of warning from that wisest of men, Solomon, runs like this: "Like the crackling of thorns under the pot, so is the laughter of fools" (Ecclesiastes 7:6). Surely, in an age of emptiness, of canned laughter blaring at us every time we turn on the television, we need to be aware that laughter without substance, or laughter at that which makes God sad or angry, can only dry out our souls and leave us parched and burned in spirit. The new Christians at Ephesus were explicitly told that there should be in their conversation nothing of "obscenity, foolish talk or coarse joking" (Ephesians 5:4).

I find myself painfully embarrassed as I recognize the astute observation made by contemporary writers, like Robertson Davies, about the behavior of Christians. He describes in horrible, accurate detail a going-away party for a girl from a fundamentalist home. Her family and church friends are gathered, and the outsider who has come is aware that "dancing was out, and there must be no jokes mentioning drink or sex. Jokes about the excretory functions would be acceptable, however, and he made two, which were greeted with loud laughter.... The party began to go swimmingly—so well, in fact that [the outsider] felt it was safe to make a joke about drink, and did so. No one laughed so loudly as [the] Pastor...."[4]

Surely the same standard that was set for the Ephesian Christians in the midst of their degraded and immoral society should apply to the humor enjoyed by Christians today. We should join in wholesome, holy laughter freely, but turn away from any laughter in which the sinless Son of God could not share.

That's easier said than done, I know. Our whole social conversation is polluted with double entendre and words of debased coinage. Being "as shrewd as snakes and as innocent as doves" (Matthew 10:16) is a necessity, and a formula for spiritual and social survival.

My dad, who spent his working life in office management and sales, had a particularly gracious way of dealing with an offensive, off-color joke. "You know, my friend," he would say, "I once thought that kind of thing was funny, too. But then I met Someone who touched all of life with such beauty that I can't joke like that anymore. His name is Jesus—and sometime I'd be glad to tell you about how I came to know Him."

Sharing the Gift

Probably the best way to be sure that you give and share in the gift of laughter in a free and clear way is simply to resist any urge to *try* to be funny or amusing.

As a classroom teacher, I have learned to look out for groaners—the kind of dull jokes which kids quickly characterize as "teacher's humor." Preachers, too, need to be aware of trying the patience of a captive audience with worn-out jokes. Actually, most serious attempts at being funny turn out to be anything but humorous. There are few people who can tell a "canned joke" well, and few occasions call for that kind of humor. I am, of course, revealing a personal prejudice. I am one of those persons who has forgotten a joke while I am still laughing at it. Punch lines elude me. The last time I tried telling a joke I completely missed the "plant," so that when I got to the punch line, the whole thing collapsed.

About the only thing I can say in self-defense is that I know I can't tell a joke, and so I stick with just enjoying life.

Training yourself to see the funny side of a situation makes life a lot more fun. Picturing your own ridiculousness in a situation is a good place to start. I can remember walking down a city street as a young woman feeling particularly smart in my navy dress. Suddenly, with a sinking sensation, I felt something cool around my ankles. I just happened to be opposite a plate glass window in which I could see a deep flounce of white below my dark skirt. The elastic in my half-slip had snapped, and my slip had slipped. Because I could see how ridiculous it looked, I could hardly repress the giggles as I stepped swiftly out of the silky cloth and then, in one motion, swooped it up with my hand and stuffed it all firmly into my handbag. Humiliating? Of course. Funny? Only if you could act as an outsider looking in.

Needless to say, the best humor pokes fun at your own foibles rather than at those of others. Let your own weaknesses provoke laughter; let the weaknesses of other people provoke compassion and concern. I am never impressed with a joke told at the expense of an ethnic group of which the teller is not a part. Nobody should tell Polish jokes except a Pole. Nor should anyone tell a joke on the Baptists unless he is a totally immersed, card-carrying member. It is just not fitting to let our laughter be at others' expense.

If you do have a story to share, learn to be brief. "Shaggy dog stories" belong to the bored and the boring. Cut out the unnecessary details: "It was Tuesday, I believe, because I can remember that I had turned the page on the calendar and had suddenly realized that I had forgotten to get a birthday card in the mail...and you know how she is about getting those birthday cards. Well, anyway, where was I?"

Drive for the part of the story where the chuckle is located.

If, in the natural course of conversation, if in sharing the joy and the fun of life, you discover that you have a gift of inducing laughter, use it to cheer others, to lighten the way, to aid digestion. But use that gift as one who will give account for "every careless word" before the Father in heaven (Matthew 12:36). And if you are not funny, that's fine too. Just join in the celebration of laughter with others.

Laughing for Health and Wholeness

"A cheerful heart is good medicine," the Proverbs tell us (Proverbs 17:22). As we come to understand more of the ways in which the human body is equipped to handle illness, I'm sure there will be increasing attention paid to the therapy of laughter.

In *Anatomy of An Illness* (New York: Norton, 1979) Norman Cousins tells how he applied this proverb in a self-prescribed treatment for a serious degenerative disease. The prognosis for his case was gradual paralysis leading to death. But Cousins fought back, and one of his main weapons was laughter.

I am convinced that, even more effective than an apple a day, is a chuckle a day. As I was breaking out of the grip of my allergic response to tobacco smoke, I discovered that a mealtime of happy laughter with friends could do more to break up the congestion in my lungs than the strongest medicine the doctors could prescribe. I would cough clear and be well for another few days. For me, laughter was one of the healing methods that God used.

One of the most severe psychiatric problems that people encounter is that of old-age depression. All the canned laughter of the television cannot bring real cheer into the heart. But a friend with whom to chuckle, a chance to join in at a table of goofy, wound-up children—these are important and within our power to provide.

Laughter is a gift given to help us survive, and to teach us that we can only survive together. The human condition with all its contradictions—its obvious mortality and its intimations of immortality, its reach constantly exceeding its grasp—is truly a risible one. The best laughter, the laughter that can heal, the laughter that has the truest ring, is the laughter that flows out of a love for life and its Giver, out of a sheer, delighted awareness of grace, and out of a healthy sense of the ridiculousness of all human posturing and pretension.

Whether we are gifted to create the humor at which others laugh, or whether we are just those who join in the shout of holy laughter, we give the gift to each other.

4

The Gift of Tears

He was a big man—six-foot-two and over 200 pounds. He had a laugh that rattled the windows. And sometimes furniture gave a sharp cracking sound when he sat down. He was our pastor, a young man with that rare gift I call a "shepherd heart." We will never forget the day he called on us just as the loss of our business had become a painful certainty. We were bewildered, confused, heartbroken. And that young pastor put his head down on his arms on the kitchen table and wept with us.

The gift of his tears, his weeping *with* us, his entering into our perplexity and sorrow, is a gift we will never forget. We loved him before that moment, but after that time a bond had been forged that will outlast these lives.

Of course, tears are a gift which must be received in love or they are indeed wasted. We need to be open to the genuine gift of tears. Shed for ourselves, they afford the release of tension, the purging of deep emotion. Shed for others, they express the genuine awareness of caring expressed through honest tears.

With the new emphasis in medicine on the body's own healing resources, tears as well as laughter will come to be better understood as the gift they truly are. But centuries of folk-wisdom have affirmed that tears are a source of healing through the release of tension, through the sense of catharsis, or through the renewal which accompanies true repentance. However, before learning to share this gift, to "mourn with those who mourn" (Romans 12:15), we may first have to learn how to cry alone.

Crying Alone

"Laugh," the old adage runs, "and the world laughs with you. Cry, and you cry alone." Sometimes crying alone is a necessary therapy. I remember one night when tears simply broke from somewhere deep within me and helped me come to a new point of stabilization. I had gone back to teaching school, sharing Cam's job with him by teaching during the farming months. And I was finding myself exhausted. Not only did I seem more tired than I should have been, but I seemed to be full of resentment. Even Cam's concern for my health made me angry. I felt I was being seen as an indispensable piece of farm equipment, necessary for spring work, but fragile and rather undependable.

I felt angry, upset, frustrated. And alone.

I had been praying, for some days, "Please, Lord, show me what is sapping my energy. Show me why I am unable to cope." And one night the answer came. I sat down on the back stairs in the low golden sunlight of early evening, and suddenly my misery dissolved into tears. Talk about having a "good cry"! I cried there alone for more than an hour. At first there was just a general welling up of misery and fatigue and discouragement and anger. And then, gradually, thoughts began to become a bit more orderly. As I sobbed quietly into the gathering night, I came through to a new understanding of myself, of why I was experiencing so much fatigue.

I realized that I was tired not just from teaching but also from a load of self-martyrdom and heroism that I had been carrying. I realized that my expectation to succeed—spectacularly, if possible—was another crushing load to be laid down. And yet another was my demand that Cam should be grateful to me—excessively so. I was carrying loads that I did not have to. That night, as I cried, one by one I laid down those extra, energy-taking loads.

Many times I have had to cry through to clarity and understanding, as though tear-washed eyes see more clearly into the heart.

Crying With God

One morning I began to pray the Lord's Prayer. Where better to start, as I awaited an answer to my request, "Lord, teach me to pray"? And that morning the glory and wonder of the prayer gripped me at an entirely new level, a spiritual rather than an intellectual one. And when I came to the phrase "Give us this day our daily bread" (usually a perfunctory request in view of the generous provision which we enjoy), I suddenly realized the phrase was "Give us...our daily bread." This was the Family Prayer of the entire church—the whole family in heaven and earth. The request was not to be made just for my well-fed family. It was for all my brothers and sisters—those hungry in famine; those in prison, deprived of all that I take to be "rights"; those, in fact, everywhere who named the Name that day and needed His provision. As I sensed the hurting Father-heart of God for these His children, I prayed in a whole new dimension, weeping as I shared their need. That day I realized in a new way my connection to the Body, and to its Head, and Heart.

There are other kinds of tears that I have not known as others have—tears of grief at bereavement, for example. But of course they too will be mine.

Grief at sin, the "gift of repentance," that painful, healing gift, was a gift that I waited long to know. As a child who reached out in love for the gift of grace in Jesus Christ, I did not experience a sudden turning or spectacular conversion. One of my own children recently commented on a song with the words, "I can remember the feeling of guilt in my soul."

"I can't," was her simple comment.

I know how she feels. As a young person, I heard more about repentance than I ever experienced. Of course I was sorry when I did wrong, but I was well trained and certainly knew how a Christian should act.

Mine were the subtler sins of the spirit. And the gift of pain that has been mine in the last ten years has been the mirror of the Word held up, again and again, to my own shallowness, my own continuous falling short, my own meanness and narrowness of spirit. And with that gift has come the gift of repentance.

Of course, the gift is not merely the tears, but the "godly sorrow" that prompts them. John Donne wrote that he could love "her who still weeps with spungie eyes / and her who is dry corke, and never cries."[1] I am sure that God loves weepers and nonweepers equally. It's not the weeping but the turning around on the heels of our lives that is the real stuff of repentance. Repentance is "good grief." It is the opposite of remorse. Remorse says, "If only—"Repentance squares its shoulders and says, "Next time, by the grace of God." Remorse is just a step away from despair, since the past cannot be changed. It leads, finally, to the Devil's damning whisper, "Despair...and die."[2] Repentance, on the other hand, is the first step toward hope. It cries out, "I shall yet live." Judas experienced remorse, and hanged himself. Peter knew repentance, and went on living in the freedom of his Lord's forgiveness and restoring love.

To live in sniffling self-condemnation is to fail to grasp the glory of forgiveness, the power of the healing Christ to say, "Your sins are forgiven...get up, take your mat and go home" (Matthew 9:2,6). Satan is appropriately called "the accuser of our brothers" (Revelation 12:10), for he delights to see God's children weeping over their sins and shortcomings—as long as their tears are those of remorse and despair. At him we fling the challenge, "Who will bring any charge against those whom God has chosen?" (Romans 8:33).

I came to understand that passage in a new way last summer, when friends of ours lost a daughter in a vehicle accident. It seemed an unnecessary sort of accident, with the vehicle Diedre was a passenger in leaving the road and rolling. Diedre, just turned 16, was flung out of the truck and died there in the ditch. The community, understandably enough, felt anger mixed with their sorrow as they gathered for the 16-year-old's funeral. As the school gym filled with people, I noticed that our friends had invited the young people who had been driving the vehicle to sit with the family in the reserved mourners' rows. And then, partway through a thoroughly jubilant, deeply Christian "celebration of the passing," the minister in charge said quietly, "The father of Diedre has asked that he might say a few words."

Don stepped forward, noticeably aged by the suffering of the previous days. He spoke quietly and with total control. "We thank you for gathering in love to remember our daughter. We want you to know that we are confident that she is at home with the Lord, and that we will meet her in His presence one day. Diedre's mother and I want it to be known that we hold nothing against any of the young people who were involved in the accident. We believe that the will of the Lord has been accomplished—and while we do not understand why, we rest in that assurance."

Suddenly I understood what Paul meant when he asserted, "Who will bring any charge against those whom God has chosen? It is God who justifies" (Romans 8:33). For those young people had, by the virtue of our friend's love and forgiveness, come under his protection. Who in the community cared to accuse those whom the father of the dead girl had forgiven? His love was their protection; the price he had paid was his right to offer such a covering.

And so it is with us. We need to grieve over sins that wound so loving a Father. But then we need to dry our eyes and step out in the confidence that, when we "confess our sins, He is faithful and just and will forgive us our sins and purify us from all unrighteousness" (I John 1:9). Then protected by His forgiveness even while awed at its cost, we go out into life assured of acceptance, assured of His love. Life begins again.

Crying Together

Tears are not only a gift for self-healing; they are a gift to be shared with others. We can share that gift first by teaching it to our children. We need to teach them that there is no shame in tears, although they are better shed privately than publicly. Let us teach our children how to let tears empty their hearts of sadness and confusion and, most important of all, of bitterness. Let us relearn, with them, how to be as emotionally honest as the psalmist, unafraid to express sorrow and anger in prayer, unafraid of tears.

Of course, we must resist the tendency on the part of anyone to use tears manipulatively. One can almost imagine the disgust with which Jesus pushed through the crowd of professional mourners when he went to heal Jairus's daughter. Paul reminds us that "Love must be sincere" (Romans 12:9). Tears, too. In order to "mourn with those who mourn" we must feel what they feel. We cannot, dare not, fake it.

My friend Sheryn was very involved in raising purebred Pomeranians at the same time that I was very involved in raising infants. She didn't much like a houseful of small children, and I didn't much like a houseful of small dogs. But somehow, across our differences, we built an enduring friendship. One day, busy with children, I felt a strong inner urging to drive up to Sheryn's house. It was quite a job to collect four little children, make sure everyone had his shoes on the right feet, wipe noses as necessary, and pile them all into the old brown Chevy. We arrived at Sheryn's gate just in time to see her running across the yard, a prized Pomeranian dog just a pile of gold fur in her arms. In the instant before my arrival, she had seen the little dog fall over and die.

I took Sheryn, still holding her dog, into my arms and cried with her. Somehow, God communicated her sorrow, her loss, to my heart—and I felt her grief. Since Sheryn was "without hope and without God in the world" (Ephesians 2:12), the loss was stunning. Something she had dared to love had died.

In the days that followed, as we talked through her grief, I was able to share with Sheryn what made life—and death—make sense to me. And only a few weeks later she opened her life to the life of Jesus Christ and let His love flood her forlorn and empty heart.

Grieving with another person sanctions his grief. It tells the person, "It's O.K. to cry." Grief is a legitimate emotion which needs expression. We live in a world where people are continuously told to "buck up." We tell our children, perhaps too often, "Chin up." We paste on little happy faces and sing false little songs about how happy we are since we know Jesus. But, as the writer of Ecclesiastes knew, there is a "time to weep" (Ecclesiastes 3:4). That time, whenever it occurs in our lives, if shared with a caring person, becomes a blessing, a gift of love.

Tears, shared or alone, are a gift from God. Jeremiah was not ashamed to shed them. Nor was Jesus. And neither should we be. We should not be ashamed of our own tears or embarrassed by the tears of others. Meanwhile, we look forward to a day when "He will wipe away every tear from [our] eyes. There will be no more death or mourning or crying or pain" (Revelation 21:4). The One who bore our sins also "carried our sorrows" (Isaiah 53:4), and it is through and because of His self-giving that someday we will enter into joy without sorrow. Until then, we will share this cup together—a token of our communion with the sorrowing, compassionate Christ and with each other.

5

The Gift of Words

The wedding party gathered on the wide lawn, occasionally glancing hopefully upward to see if the mist was going to lift. It was easy to see who were the optimists and who were the pessimists. The optimists had sunglasses pushed up in their hair. The pessimists had umbrellas. But although the sun did not actually break out enough for the sunglasses set, neither did the mist resolve into a drizzle decided enough for the umbrella-carriers. The young couple exchanged their vows under the big sheltering trees, and later, after lunch, I was asked to say a few words to them.

In the days of once-upon-a-time,
when people gathered to celebrate momentous
occasions such as this,
there was always a hushed moment
when the good fairies gave their gifts.

As I thought of saying a few words
at this event, I wondered:

If I were a Good Fairy
(which I assuredly am not)
and could grant this couple
one very special gift,
what would I give them
on this their wedding day?

I turned away from many gifts
that suggested themselves to me.

But now I know:
I would grant to you both
the gift of words.

I would wish your marriage to be filled
with the ongoing conversation of two aware persons
who seek to enflesh their ideas, their love,
their being in words.

I would grant you words
in which to give birth to your feelings of love.
Do not be mute—
Say "I love you" a thousand different ways.

I would grant you words
in which to robe your dreams,
and words to wrap around your griefs.

I would grant you words when you are angry or hurt
(but careful words, so that anger and hurt are not
multiplied),
and words when you are sad and disappointed.
And I would say to each of you—
Say it...speak it...embody it in words.

Let your marriage be full of talk.

The Gift of Conversation

It is a sign of the impoverishment of ideas that a word
which at one time meant deep, ongoing conversation has
come to mean only the physical act of sex. Intercourse—in
its richest, fullest, broadest meaning—should encompass all
of life lived together.

The gift of conversation, of deep, thoughtful word-sharing,

is one needed not only in marriage but in any deep and abiding friendship. I was glad to hear a young couple include, after exchanging traditional wedding vows, their own more-informal exchange, which included each saying to the other, "I love you dearly and I want to share my life with you. You are my best friend."

Our noisy, media-dominated environment works against our relearning the skill of pleasant, easily flowing, give-and-take conversation. We start the day with the radio giving us the bad news and weather. In the evenings we grunt and exchange a few words between television shows. And we never really get to know the people we live with.

My son gave me a painful lesson in the art of conversation while I was driving him to music lessons one day. I complained about his reading a magazine. "I had though we might have this time to chat," I said.

"We are," he said, distractedly looking up from the magazine. "I learned the art of conversation from my mother."

Since then I have tried to be more disciplined in laying aside print in order to be with people, especially the very special people in my own family. For I am aware that learning to talk together is important for us all. Single or married, young or old, we need to talk, to share ourselves, to listen. We need intercourse—in its old-fashioned, Oxford English Dictionary sense of the word.

Find a Place, Make a Space

Conversation grows best in a space that is specially set aside for it. Many people fail to realize how crowded their marriage has become with the concerns of children, and how little time they really have to talk with each other. Couples need to go out for dinner; friends need to make a date for a few minutes in a quiet teahouse in order to rediscover each other.

A home that is built around the importance of conversation makes space for talk. It means a television set that is turned off unless a specific, chosen program is being watched, and that even this gives way in priority to people. If guests arrive, the television goes off with a snap. It means, as my father used to say, children who know how to "run along now and sell your papers."

Table talk, that special interchange of ideas among the members of a family, is facilitated by a table big enough for everyone. How we enjoy our big trestle table! I wish it could record deep in its pine boards the laughter and chatter of the children, the sparkle and freshness of the conversation of our guests, and then play it all back at some quieter, less people-filled stage of our lives.

Homes built to function around the television set and the bar counter deny the importance of gathering and the significance of conversation. In the same way, homes that are dominated by mouthy little children also work against meaningful talk.

But no matter how well-adapted the home is to conversation, all of us treasure times of conversation in quietly elegant or quaintly different places, times when two or three or four people have set aside a space and a time just to be together, to talk.

A friend recently gave Cam and me the compliment of a little parchment that is now tacked to the bulletin board above my desk: "A happy marriage is a long conversation that always seems too short."[1] Exactly. After 20 years of marriage, we find that all of life has become one long conversation that flows on from day to day. We visit, habitually. When we come in from work, we have a cup of coffee and debrief each other. That's just a warm-up for the special pot-of-tea time after the children have been excused from our noisy and exuberant supper table. We have tried to make our whole lives a space and our whole home a place for conversation—between ourselves and with others.

Ask a Question

Some people think that if they are great talkers, they are

great conversationalists. Actually, except for specially gifted raconteurs, most talkers are just great bores. Conversation must be two-way to be worth anything at all. It is in fact the perfect example of the way in which giving and receiving are reciprocal. In true conversation, sound must interplay with silence, and talking with careful, attentive listening. The first gift of a conversationalist is not the gift of speaking, but of listening. The best conversations start with a question: "How was your day?" Or, "What's on your heart?" Or, "Where are you hurting?"

I remember how I used to look forward to a Sunday-morning conversation with Reta. She was several years older than I, her children down the path from mine. But she always sought me out for a little visit after church. I went home one day trying to analyze why I enjoyed visiting with her so much. And I made a discovery: I enjoyed Reta because she seemed genuinely interested in me, in my week, in my ideas. And she loved to laugh with me. "Cheer up!" she used to encourage. "I though we'd never get to the time when we could travel without a potty, but here we are!" She met me where I was and placed herself close to my young-wife/young-mother concerns, offering a sharing, caring heart, and I love her dearly for it.

One of the great compensations of growing older is that friendships get longer, reaching back through hours of happy conversation sprinkled through years of memories. There are a number of special friends with whom we visit infrequently, but with whom each time the conversation seems like a piece of knitting that has been temporarily laid aside to be picked up and continued.

Each year between Christmas and New Year's we visit with our special friends, Isabelle and Ray. We are continuing a tradition of once-a-year visits that we have shared with them for probably 15 seasons. We have sat together in our several farm homes, in the light of kerosene lanterns specially lit for the evening, by candlelight, or, as this year, in cozy, quiet lamplight. Together we have talked through everything from parenting to midlife crises. We have shared ideas, discussed goals, cried, laughed, and prayed together.

For us, conversation with Christian friends just naturally blends into prayer. With our closest friends we just naturally pray around the circle of our conversation before we say goodbye.

We were just learning to make this a habit some years ago when a special friend was visiting with us. "Let's pray," Cam said simply as the conversation drew to a close. Our friend told us later how it had felt to him:

"I was used to praying out of a prayer book. I don't know if I had ever uttered a spontaneous prayer in public before. Cam started to pray, and he prayed long. Maxine prayed, and she prayed longer. And then there was a silence and I knew it was my turn. I broke into a sweat and managed to stammer through one sentence. But I survived—and prayer has never been the same since."

For us, binding our conversation in prayer seems the natural way to say goodbye. It presents our words, our lives, our friendship, and our conversation before the Father for His special blessing. Sometimes we pray something like, "Lord, blow over this conversation with the breath of your Spirit. Whatever is good and comes from You, please place it deep in our hearts. Whatever is spurious, blow it away like chaff."

Share a Book

One of the special ways of acknowledging the gift of words is through sharing a book with a friend. A book that says something special to you becomes a treasure to the friend to whom it is loaned or given. Sometimes I read a book that speaks so clearly on an issue of great importance that I buy several and give them to special friends. (I would much rather *give* a book than *loan* one. Loaned books have a way of mysteriously disappearing.)

Sometimes I share a good book through a quotation shared in a letter, or even by merely suggesting the title to a bookstore-haunting friend. I love to get letters in which friends share with me what they are reading, what books are shaping and sharpening their thoughts.

My children have wonderfully opened their world of special books to me, and I have shared favorites from childhood with them. With my children I have explored the books of Elizabeth Goudge and Madeleine L'Engle and Lois Lenski. With them I have revisited the wonderful *House at Pooh Corners* (made more wonderful than ever by their laughter) and have reentered the solemn delights of *The Secret Garden*. There is someting magical in this kind of sharing—an opening to each other of special worlds.

Write a Note

In one of the children's favorite Richard Scarry books, the little phrase occurs, "If I write a letter to someone I love/ someone I love may write a letter to me."[2] It is in this hope that I write letters, and cherish the ones I receive. The children have also begun to enjoy pen-friends, and their notes and letters are added to the outgoing and incoming mail.

In the pell-mell pace of our lives, sustaining a number of friendships through the thoughtful conversation of personal correspondence requires some discipline and dedication. Since I am personally addicted to the delight of getting mail, I cultivate a few special ongoing conversations by mail. These are letters that I read and reread, that I spread out before the Lord and pray over, that I play with in my mind and finally make reply to. It has been through some of these special friendships-by-correspondence that key ideas have been formulated, leading into books or articles.

I am sure that none of my regular correspondents could accuse me of overwhelming them with letters, although one sure way to kill a correspondence is to "overwrite." The other sure way to kill one, of course, is to "underwrite." A slow, steady pace of exchange of letters—perhaps a letter received one month and replied to the next—works best for my personal correspondence. That gives me time to really enjoy the previous letter, to savor the ideas in it, and to let new ideas formulate. I value most those letters which challenge me with ideas and tempt me to read new books, but I love to hear about anything my friends are doing.

Letter-writing is one way of "journalizing," of capturing something from the flow of life. Carbon copies kept on file become part of one's ongoing record of personal growth and thought.

Whether they are conversations across distance, conversations across time, or conversations across the table, how I treasure the intercourse of ideas, the interplay of wit and fun, the interchange of concern which is the gift of words! As a writer, I especially treasure the trust of the words of the English language. Ordering words in meaningful patterns, in everything from conversation to books, means cooperating with the Spirit who brought cosmos from chaos. It means working with One who is in Person the Creative, Sustaining, Redeeming Word. And so with the psalmist I pray, "May the words of my mouth and the meditation of my heart be pleasing in your sight, O Lord, my Rock and my Redeemer" (Psalm 19:14).

6

The Gift of Silence

I think it was the discovery of silence that made moving out to our farm significant to me. The night we first slept in the old home place, I lay wakeful in a strange bedroom under the sloping attic roof, a room awash in the silver light of a full moon. In that late autumn night I could hear the faint yelping of coyotes and the soft insistent call of an owl. All my life I had read of owls "hooting." Now I knew how short the words fell as a description of that muted, pulsating call.

I have had several thousand still farm nights to enjoy since that one—nights that roar with the sound of the wind in the spruce trees or shout the exultation of spring in the wild rush of water through our ravine, nights that thrill with the shrill piping of frogs or fill suddenly with the nearing call of homing geese, nights of perfect silence under the rippling curtains of northern lights.

And I have found that the more I have learned to enjoy

the quiet of the countryside, the less tolerant I have become of meaningless, demanding noise. At the same time I am sure that the quiet that really matters is an inner stillness, something which some people are able to cultivate in the middle of a throbbing city or a screaming factory. Whether or not we are granted the gift of outer silence, the gift of inner silence can be ours to have and to share.

The Companionship of Silence

Much as I treasure the gift of words, I also enjoy the companionship of those special few people with whom I can enjoy silence. There are not many, of course—people with whom I can walk across a pasture, now talking, now just quietly absorbing the beauty, the quiet, the companionship.

My idea of a nearly perfect evening is one spent with another person or two in a warm, lamplit, book-lined room, each reading a book, pausing once in a while to interrupt each other with an idea, and finally sitting down to a pot of tea to talk over the books, the ideas, the insights of the evening. The companionableness of silence is a very special one, and one which we can learn to give each other.

The Comfort of Silence

Faced with life's great mysteries of pain and bereavement, we struggle to find words. I know that I have "indefinitely postponed" visits I ought to have made, just because I wasn't sure what I should say at such a time. Maybe, when we don't know what to say, we should just say nothing. We should offer the gift of our presence in perfect silence, expressing by being there our concern and our love. So often, in groping for words, we say things that hurt rather than heal. Sometimes silence would be better.

Recently I heard a man tell his story of responding to Jesus Christ. He was more than 50 years old before he responded to the good news of God's love for him with his own personal "Yes." And yet, as a young boy, he had witnessed his own father's deathbed conversion; he had been taken to

Sunday school by his mother; he had been aware of his mother's lifelong prayers for his salvation. Why had it taken so long for him to respond?

"I'm not accusing," he says quietly, "and I know I used this thing as an excuse for many years. But when my daddy died in the early days of the Great Depression, leaving behind him a wife with seven children, the preacher tried to comfort us. 'Your father was such a fine man,' he said, 'that God decided He needed him in heaven more than you needed him here.' The words were kindly meant, but as a boy of ten I found myself hating a God who would think He needed my daddy more than I did. And it took years and years to get over the bitterness planted that day."

His story is by no means unique. Our simplistic explanations for things that defy us with their mystery do God no favor. Far better to say nothing, or to admit that we do not understand why some things happen.

Last summer we attended the funeral of one of Cam's classmates. As a young woman she had struggled to raise her family alone. Then, just at the time when life looked like it could open out onto something besides sheer struggle, it was all over. As we left the funeral, I overheard two men talking. "Nothing can make this make sense." They were right. There simply were no easy answers. These are times that call for silence.

These are times when, like Job's comforters, we are probably at our best just to sit down in silence. It is when we start trying to explain that we get into trouble.

The Joy of Solitude

For those of us who live in constant close fellowship with others, the joy of solitude is often a rare one. Probably the person in our society with the least time of solitude is the young mother in the home. I remember wondering if I would ever again be able to have a bath without someone calling urgently at the door, obviously needing the bathroom far more than I did at that particular moment. In fact, memories of those days make me smile when time-management experts tell us to differentiate between the urgent and the important. I'm sure it's a good principle, all right, but for a mother with preschoolers, the urgent and the important are usually the same thing.

Now, of course, the little callers are gone from the door. I just have to hope that the telephone doesn't ring while I'm in the tub. How in this world do we find solitude?

A few years ago I came to the end of the school term in which I had been teaching. I was tired, exhausted of anything like creativity, and feeling as spiritually dried out as a well-squeezed sponge. I announced to the Lord: "This is the summer I am going to have some time alone with You." I envisioned long, slow walks, alone with the Lord, across the back pasture, out to where the river curves and bends its way through green shrubs and close-cropped pasture, to sit on a great, glaciated boulder and think, and pray, and be.

But such was not to be. The days were busy and people-filled. The one or two chances I did get to walk out across the pasture, I had friends or family along. It was a good summer, but not one filled with the solitude I had yearned for.

That summer the Lord taught me how to have inner stillness in the midst of outer clamor. Just one psalm, read again and again, was the source of my meditation that summer: Psalm 138. "The Lord will fulfill his purpose for me" (Psalm 138:8) became my resting point. Not silence but stillness became my portion, so that one day I could write—

> I celebrate stillness, not silence:
> Hawk-scream, fly-buzz, river-pluck, bird-chat,
> And my dog's rhythmic panting.
> I celebrate stillness, not silence:
> Child-shout, dinner-laughter, dish-clatter,
> And appliances chugging.
> Not silence,
> but life-sounds,
> cupped in this stillness within.

The gift of silence is one which we can give each other:

by respecting each other's need for space and place to be alone with God; by offering to look after children so a young mother can have a few hours alone; by learning when our friends have their special "silent times" and avoiding calling them at that time.

And silence is a gift we need to work at giving ourselves. One young father I know, living in a mobile home with a wife and family of four small children, gets up at 5:45 in the morning to have time with the Lord. Where does he meditate and pray? "In the bathroom," he confesses. "It's the only place where I can be really alone."

Most people who have entered into the joy of silent times in God's presence tell of the struggle to clear that space. In my experience, accustomed as I am to interruption and sharing of my time, the time that I set aside for silence often becomes clamorous with internal claims on my attention, and I discover that the real enemy of silence is not the things outside myself but those inside.

I was comforted to find Henri Nouwen state that this is a common problem for those who seek to develop silence and solitude: "As soon as we are alone, without people to talk with, books to read, TV to watch, or phone calls to make, an inner chaos opens up in us. This chaos can be so disturbing and so confusing that we can hardly wait to get busy again.... Time in solitude may at first seem little more than a time in which we are bombarded by thousands of thoughts and feelings that emerge from hidden areas of our mind.... At first, the many distractions keep presenting themselves. Later, as they receive less and less attention, they slowly withdraw."[1]

As a beginner in the practice of solitude—or perhaps a relearner, having loved solitary hours with God as a teenager, but having lost time to call my own during the childbearing and early nurture years—I can affirm that it takes time and practice to clear a few minutes of distractions so that we can focus on God and on His Word. But the reward of being in His presence, of having the Spirit of

God open the Word of God to us—that is so great a thrill that we are drawn back, again and again, to that "inner room" of secret solitude.

Sharing the Gift of Silence

Like so many good gifts, the gift of silence is not well-apportioned in our world. Many people have too much silence: the elderly, the hospitalized, the people who live alone. And many people have too little. A gateway for a ministry of love might be to consider ways in which to "swap silence." I remember the response of a single friend of ours when we offered him the use of a little guest house on our farm. "Anytime you would like to come," we told him, "you can have the little house all to yourself."

We thought we were offering something special—certainly something that would sound good to us!

But our friend turned down our offer with some spirit. "Of house all to myself I have plenty," he said. "I come here for the chat and laughter of family. Just make up the bed in the laundry room for me and I am perfectly happy."

And so we invite friends who have much aloneness into the noisy, interrupted conversation that is family. Equally, friends who have a lot of silence could offer to swap an evening of silence for one of sound by exchanging homes with a young couple for an evening or overnight once in a while...a treat going both ways. I can imagine the blessing that a mature but lonely woman could be to a hassled young mother if she would say: "I'll come one afternoon a week and look after the kids and put supper on. And you can go to my apartment and sleep, or read a book, or spend time in prayer." The giving and receiving would be fully mutual.

Silence is for some people the long-sought-after golden state; for others, the burden of life. If we could find ways to share it more fully, both as burden and blessing, we would simultaneously give and receive one of the great boons of life.

The Gift of Prayer

Close cousin to the gift of silence is the gift of prayer. Here is one gift you can give without anybody but your Father in heaven knowing you have given it. Years ago I learned (from a now-forgotten book) a technique of prayer which gives me great joy. It is simply to raise people and situations into the presence of God for His blessing as we encounter them: the parking lot attendant; the girl in the next office; the people in the elevator with me. None of them know that I have brought them to the Father, but I have given them a silent love-gift.

I often pray for neighbors as I drive down our country roads, naming specific needs if I know them, or just asking God to work in that home by His Holy Spirit. I pray when a friend's name or face presents itself to my mind, lifting that person by name for the Father's blessing. And, of course, I love to be like the mothers of Salem and bring my children to our Lord, one by one, for His love and benediction.

There are, of course, many times when the gift of prayer can be given directly by praying with the person: when a friend brings me a problem or a grief or a dream to consider, we often clasp hands or lock ourselves in each other's arms and pray about the whole matter—lifting ourselves, our minds, and our problems together to the One who can help us.

I have been greatly blessed by those who have prayed for me. When my parents were involved in a serious car accident a number of years ago, the thing that nearly shattered me was the thought that, had they been taken "home," I would have been without their prayers. How much I need to know that they are lifting me and my family to the Lord day by day. And one of the greatest blessings that has come my way through my writing is that, here and there, someone has been moved to pray for me on a regular basis. These prayer friends offer me a very special gift, and one for which I am most grateful.

I remember a hot August afternoon several years ago when I was on my way to Edmonton for surgery. I was sitting in the car outside our small-town hospital, silent and taut under the demands of pain. Cam was inside picking up my doctor's notes and X-rays to take with us. There was a little tap at my window, and I looked up, surprised to see the round, anointed-looking face of the local parish priest, looking in at me with care and concern.

Quickly I pressed the switch and the window slid down. "Hello, Father Beauvoir."

"Hello," he said, his voice full of that ineffable sweetness that I might, on another day, have called affection. Today I was in no mood to judge. "I met your husband in the hospital and he tells me you are on your way to Edmonton."

"Yes," I nodded, wondering at his concern. Believer though I was, I was not one of his parishioners.

"You have been sick for some time?" he asked.

"All summer," I shrugged. The pain nudged me, reminding me of its presence.

"I will bless you," he said. Swiftly he raised his hand, his fingers sketching a cross in the air. Its shape hung between us as he chanted in a rapid, high-pitched drone, "In the name of the Father, Son, and Holy Ghost." And then, without pausing for even a slip of breath, he said, with a suddenly bright smile, "You will be all right."

Suddenly I knew that I would be. His prayer and his prophecy had not told me something I did not know, but confirmed what I already believed. I would take to the city— along with the sealed manila envelope containing X-rays and diagnostic notes, along with the nudging, edging, singeing, surging pain in my side—the smile of happy confidence with which the priest had ended his blessing, and the air-hung sign of the cross.

I was deeply moved by his pausing to pray for me, and my faith was built by his words of encouragement. "Pray for each other" (James 5:16). It should be as natural, as habitual, and as without fanfare as Father Beauvoir's blessing. It should be one of the gifts we offer without self-consciousness to other people as we perceive their needs.

7

The Gifts of Encouragement And Rebuke

Just recently I received a letter from a very special woman with whom I had been out of touch for many years. She was a person who had, without question, the gift of sharp rebuke. As an InterVarsity Christian Fellowship staff member, she had touched my life while I was a student in both high school and university. She stung me with her criticism of my close, tight grip on all truth and propriety.

"We evangelicals," she would say sharply, "are the counterpart to the Pharisees of Jesus' day, you know." My anger matched theirs.

She smashed away at my smugness and spiritual pride through the years that rubbed together, two rocks in a rock tumbler, polishing each other. But despite my defensiveness, she managed to minister to me. And years later I would realize that it was her gift of rebuke, her challenge and criticism, that would enable me to be open to many of the unusual opportunitites for witness and worship which would later become a part of my life.

Hate her? Love her? Twenty years ago I might not have been sure. Today I know: I love her and thank God for her. She gave me, lovingly and without apology, the gift of rebuke. And for that I love her dearly.

Encouragement and rebuke: this gift is like a well-worn coin. On one side is a smiling face and an inscription which reads, "Strengthen [the] feeble arms and weak knees" (Hebrews 12:12). On the other side is a visage, terrible in its severity, with the inscription, "No discipline seems pleasant at the time" (Hebrews 12:11). Naturally, we turn the smiling side up first, polishing it with our finger. For who of us does not enjoy giving and receiving the gift of encouragement?

A young elementary teacher told me about how a language arts consultant had enriched her life. "She would first of all tell me about something I was doing well. And I would be so glad that I was doing something—anything—right that after this she could have told me to stand in the corner on my head, and I would have done it for her." The other young teachers around the table nodded and concurred. The woman who was their consultant was also chairman of the Teachers' Christian Fellowship retreat at which I was speaking. She was a beautiful woman who had learned how to build people by means of the gift of encouragement.

It is a gift which each of us has received, sometime, somewhere. Perhaps it was a teacher who knew how to kindle us with a smile or a nod of approval. Perhaps our parents were wise enough to know to express to us their favor—in at least equal measure with their disfavor! The more we have received this gift, the more we are open to it. One of the strange and painful facts about this gift is that the person who needs encouragement most may be the person least able to accept it, just because he has never really learned that there was anything very commendable about him. Such people are prone to brush aside an encouraging word without absorbing it into themselves, perhaps with a self-disparaging word: "You thought that was good? I thought it was a complete mess." Unconsciously, of course, they disparage the encourager as well as themselves.

In giving and receiving encouragement, we open ourselves and others to fulfilling potential. For encouragement is an acknowledgment of attempt, not necessarily a commendation on achievement. It is the offer of hope. In its spiritual sense, it begins by being able to see by faith what a person is in God's eyes and what he is capable of becoming through God's grace. Encouragement is putting that vision into words.

Encouragement is dreaming God's dreams for another person, even when those dreams are far from fulfillment. I remember how it was when Lorraine first came to know Jesus Christ as her Lord. She came to Him—and to me—with deep emotional problems. And yet, within a few weeks of her conversion, she was a sharer. First she brought her sister to know Jesus too. And then she began to tell her friends what she had found in Him

"I am going to share with you something I see," I told her one morning after our ladies' Bible study as we lunched together. "I see that you are being given the gift of evangelism. You have both the ability to communicate and the experience to communicate from, and when the Lord has healed you, you are going to have unusual opportunity to share the gospel with others." She looked at me, mystified and bewildered, her eyes still wearing the guarded, veiled look which was a symptom of her chronic depression. She could scarcely absorb what I said.

"Me?" she shrugged with a little laugh. "I don't see how that could be." At that time it was only by faith that I could see a time when she would be set free from her personal problems to minister to others.

A couple of years passed, during which Lorraine grew in grasp of the Word, and grew toward the light in her own life. And then, one Sunday, Lorraine served as substitute teacher in my husband's adult Bible class. Her preparation was so thorough, her presentation so interesting and clear, that after class another young wife in the class approached her.

"Wouldn't you like to start a morning Bible study?" she asked. "I just enjoyed your class so much this morning—I'll promise to be your first regular member." It was with that further encouragement that Lorraine began a weekly Bible study in her home in which women have been exploring the Word of God and coming to know Lorraine's Lord. The gift was clearly given by the Spirit, but it was called into action by the ministry of encouragement.

Unlike praise, which is a gift reserved for those who achieve, the gift of encouragement can be offered to the person for whom things are not going well. And often, encouragement can make the difference between despair and hope, between defeat and courage.

The gift of encouragement was given to us, very tangibly, one winter by a friend. We had sold the "home place," the farm we had bought from Cam's father ten years earlier in order to pay off debts incurred through crop failure and wipeout on the cattle market. We were back to point zero with one big question looming: dare we try farming again? Through all the long, dark winter we wondered. And then, toward spring, a few material signs of hope began to emerge.

For one thing, our major creditor encouraged us to invest a portion of the equity realized from the sale of the family farm back into land. To our amazement, we found ourselves owners of a farm once again. The question now was: a farm—for what? To resell so we could liquidate remaining debt? To rent out to someone else? Or was the land for us to farm? And if so, where would we find the operating money?

Part of the answer came one day when Cam's dad offered to lend him of part of the required operating money. And another part of it came the day that Walter stopped by.

Walter was, in our minds, the ideal farmer. He and his

wife Jeanne had raised a fine family, built a well-run farm, and done all the things we dreamed of. Though we visited back and forth once in a while, that day I didn't expect Walter. Cam was away for the day. The look on Walter's face when I answered his knock at the back door told me how sorry he was to have missed Cam. I sensed quickly that this was more than a social visit. He seemed, somehow, a bit reticent—nervous, maybe, although why I could not imagine.

I poured coffee and we small-talked...about our families, about the weather. I knew there was something more on Walter's mind.

"Well," he said finally, swallowing his last mouthful of coffee. "I actually came to tell Cam something. But I guess you could pass it on for me."

"Of course." I set the coffeepot back on the stove and sat down.

"We know what it's like to have tough times," he said. "When Jeanne and I first started out, we didn't have two nickels to rub together. Really." He paused. "One day a friend of our family's called me aside and pressed a folded 20-dollar bill into my hand. That was like, say, a thousand dollars would be today."

We sat in the silence that fell. Then Walter went on. "We used that $20 to pay off a debt. And somehow we inched our way ahead. We were finally able to sell that farm—a little patch of rocks was all it was, really, and buy better land...."

I was offering coffee again, automatically. Walter covered his mug. "No, thanks," he smiled. "I really have to be on my way. But what I came to tell Cam is this: I have a bin of cleaned barley seed—500 bushels. It's Cam's to use this spring. And when he gets his crop off this fall, he can just fill the bin up for us again." And then Walter lifted his coat off the hook behind the door and was gone.

I found myself sitting, as the afternoon fell gray and cool around me in the little kitchen, tracing around the edges of the checks on the plaid plastic tablecloth with the handle of my spoon. The full impact of the offer hit me only gradually.

I could hardly wait to share Walter's message with Cam. The dimension of his gift staggered us both. For it was far more than merely material—substantial as that aspect was. Not only did this gift mean that we could put a crop in, but, far more important, that someone we trusted and respected thought we *should* put that crop in.

We could start again. We had seed, and hope.

And that's what encouragement is all about. That, of course, is the nice side of the coin, the side with the smile, the side of the coin we like to ponder and turn up in our hands. It is fun to give encouragement and even more fun to receive it. Passing encouragement in the form of kind and uplifting words, or in the form of substantial material help, feels good to both giver and receiver.

The Gift of Rebuke

But the reverse side of this gift is also a gift which true friends give each other. It is the gift of rebuke.

Now I must be very honest: I love to give and to receive the gift of encouragement, but I am less enthusiastic about receiving—and very hesitant about giving—the gift of rebuke. It is an uncomfortable gift, awkward and hard to package. And yet it is a true gift, and an important one. "Faithful are the wounds of a friend," the Scripture says (Proverbs 27:6). Over the years I have received a number of such painful gifts, and I find that I can thank God for each one of them. One such gift was given to me as a teenager at summer camp. In the course of the week at camp I had memorized the first chapter of the Book of Hebrews. The director asked me to recite the chapter at an evening gathering. As I walked along the path toward the chapel, I remarked flippantly to one of my friends, "I'm supposed to recite the stupid old first chapter of Hebrews tonight."

One of the camp leaders happened to overhear my off-the-cuff remark. He paused and turned to me for just a flash of a moment. "Don't forget that's the Word of God you're speaking of, young lady," he said. That was all. He did not relate to me in depth. He did not rap with me. He did not, above all, apologize for what he had to say. He simply and firmly ministered the gift of rebuke.

Of course I thought I would die of embarrassment. But I learned a lesson I would never forget. That young man went on to have a fruitful pastoral ministry and later become a district superintendent in his denomination. No doubt the twin gifts of encouragement and rebuke are still important ones in his minsitry.

Cam recalls an elderly schoolteacher who drew him aside in the staff room one day when they were teaching on the same staff. She offered him a word of rebuke about a speech habit he had developed. I think, if I remember correctly, it was the addition of the very Canadian ending "eh" to most sentences. "It detracts from what you have to say, Campbell," she said firmly, in her clear, crisply articulated, schoolteachery manner. "I think you would be well-advised to curb it." Cam was rebuffed, hurt. He stung with embarrassment. But he eliminated the offensive habit and became a more poised and attractive communicator. Faithful wounds.

I suppose most of the rebukes I have received were from my parents. Perhaps their rebukes saved me from having to receive them from less loving sources. From them, too, I learned early that the ability to accept a rebuke and learn from it was the mark of wisdom. "A reproof entereth more into a wise man than an hundred stripes into a fool" (Proverbs 17:10 KJV) we used to read from Proverbs in our after-breakfast family devotions. I never found it easy to lay down my defenses and accept a rebuke. Even yet, although I know I will gain by it, I shrink from that gift.

I think with pain of loving rebukes I have failed to accept. Once a friend wrote to suggest that I dominated conversation while my husband, "who seems at least as witty and intelligent as you," was overshadowed or interrupted. I was completely unable to accept her rebuke. I wrote back an angry, defensive letter in which I excused my own behavior and then pointed out several things I had noticed about her that I didn't particularly like, either. My response was destructive—and yet, despite the pain, I *did* learn something through her rebuke.

Because I find rebuke so painful to accept, it is a gift I do not enjoy giving. There are, of course, some people who feel called to a ministry of rebuke. Most of them are not really offering a gift at all. They are merely throwing hand grenades because they enjoy explosions. There is another group who think that if they wrap a rebuke in a joke, it is easier to take. Not so. When someone's slapping my back after a joke, I like to know there is no knife in his hand. I would a hundred times rather have someone speak to me in a straightforward and sincere way about something he perceives to be a problem than to be lampooned. I am unable to respond to rebukes wrapped in jokes or sarcasm, or delivered to a whole group although intended for just one member.

A rebuke, to be acceptable, must be wrapped in love— real love and concern for the person. A rebuke should not just vent our own feelings of affront or offense, but should be directed toward helping the other person develop. "You are not ready to go to another person with a word of reproof unless you have wept over the fault you are rebuking," is the way one wise pastor puts it. The whole point of rebuke is correction and restoration. We do not rebuke others to make a point, but to help another person grow into his full stature.

Not only must a rebuke be offered straightforwardly and lovingly, but it also must be offered vulnerably. None of us needs some paragon of virtue to come and tell us how to do something better. But if someone with whom I can identify comes to me, someone who will share with me how he learned a similar painful and difficult lesson, someone who comes to me in transparent love, vulnerable to my defensive backlash, then I am humbled into accepting that rebuke.

The fairest way to minister rebuke is to go in person—as Jesus instructs—and, in a one-to-one situation share your deep concern about a behavior or habit that is diminishing the other person.

I shrink even more from giving rebukes than I do from receiving them. Yet, as the years come and go, I realize that I have learned far more through rebuke than I have through praise. Praise may do little more than confirm what I know. Rebuke usually shows me something I didn't know. Perhaps someday I will know better how to minister in love the gift of rebuke. Right now, I only know it as a painful gift that has enriched my life, and one which I pass on most tenderly.

Perhaps it is a gift into which we should mature, a gift for elders: for parents to give to their children, for teachers to give to their students, for older people to give, lovingly and without harshness, to younger people. Of one thing I am sure: it is far easier to talk about a problem behind a person's back than to confront him with the gift of rebuke. Perhaps if we denied ourselves the luxury of criticism, and disciplined ourselves to give lovingly and carefully the gift of rebuke, the church would have a stronger, clearer witness.

"Brothers, if someone is caught in a sin, you who are spiritual should restore him gently" (Galatians 6:1). There is the real qualification for ministering the gift of rebuke: it is properly the task of one who is *spiritual*—one who has spent much time in the presence of the Lord Jesus Christ absorbing His love and His tenderness as well as His anger at sin and its consequences. For all of us who must sometimes rebuke others—in our role as parents, employers, teachers, church elders, or just as older brothers and sisters in Christ—it is from Jesus that we must learn. His concern for the person never made Him tolerant of sin. But how gently He speaks to those who are most fragile: "Neither do I condemn you.... Go now and leave your life of sin" (John 8:11).

Something to consider, however, is the possibility that if we were to exercise the gift of encouragement more, we might have to exercise the gift of rebuke less. Certainly it is true in our families: positive reinforcement by thanks or appreciation vastly reduces the number of instances when negative reinforcement by punishment or rebuke must be used. No doubt it is true in the larger family, the church, as well. The young person encouraged is much less likely to become a dropout. The older person who is genuinely thanked for something may suddenly have fewer complaints. The new believer who is encouraged by fellowship and prayer will find it easier to resist temptation. How much better to *build* each other up than to *pick* each other up!

I saw an example of such encouragement being offered just the other day. Our pastor brought a couple of teenagers to a once-a-month fellowship meeting, where Christians from several churches in the area meet to praise and to pray. "I want to introduce Allan to you all," he said. "He is just one day old in the Lord. And," he said, turning to the second teenager, "this is his friend, Clay. He came to know the Lord about seven months ago." It had been just the night before, following the youth meeting, that Allan had asked Jesus Christ to become Lord of his life, encouraged to take that step by Clay's enthusiastic endorsement of Jesus.

Later in the evening, as we had dinner together, I saw Randy, a man in his early thirties, seek out the two teenagers and sit down with them. It was just a year since that young man had become a Christian, and now he was sharing his testimony with the new believers, encouraging them as Barnabas did the new believers at Antioch "to remain true to the Lord with all their hearts" (Acts 11:23). A few minutes later, when I glanced in their direction, the young men had their heads bowed close together around Randy's Bible as the one-year-old shared with the one-day-old and the seven-month-old Christians the truths on which he had built his new life. What a joy to see the ministry of encouragement in operation!

"But you, dear friends," writes that man of few words, Jude, "build yourselves up in your most holy faith and pray in the Holy Spirit. Keep yourselves in God's love as you wait for the mercy of our Lord Jesus Christ to bring you to eternal life. Be merciful to those who doubt; snatch others from the fire and save them; to others show mercy, mixed with fear" (Jude 20-23). There in summary form is the Scriptural teaching regarding the twin gifts of encouragement and rebuke.

In loving encouragement, in gentle and tender rebuke, we need to build each other up. We need constantly to find ways, places, and times to "encourage one another—and all the more as [we] see the Day approaching" (Hebrews 10:25).

8

Forgiveness—The Gift You Need to Give

~∽◦∾∽◦∾∽◦∾∽◦∾∽◦∾∽◦∾∽◦∾~

We were very hard up that winter. And so, when a neighbor offered to buy an old rubber-tired wagon, I looked forward to the $75 we had agreed upon. And looked forward to it. One day, as I wondered angrily when he would pay, I sat down to write my annual mortgage-postponement letter to Prudential. "Dear Sir," I wrote, "Could we again ask for a postponement of payment? As you are no doubt aware, the quotas have not yet opened up for delivery of wheat, and so we are unable to pay at this time." My letter went on with reassurances of our good intentions, and a suggested date for payment "at least of the interest."

I hated writing those letters, begging for clemency. But that day, as I wrote, I was interrupted by the dog's loud barking. "Oh, good," I thought. "Maybe it's Jake, come to give us a check." I scraped at the frosted window to peer out, farmer-wife-style, and as I did, the Lord spoke to me. With a sense of horror I realized how closely I had parallelled the attitude of the unmerciful servant in Jesus' parable (Matthew 18:21-35). Here I was, asking for and expecting to get a merciful postponement of an onerous payment while at the same time ready to seize my neighbor by the throat for a few dollars owing us! The dog stilled. I could see now that it was Jake, leaving the yard, the rubber-tired wagon towed behind his tired-looking pickup truck. He didn't stop at the house. "Father," I prayed, "forgive me. I'll let this thing go." Later I couldn't remember whether we were ever paid for the old wagon. But Cam tells me we still have it, so I guess Jake brought it back. I only know that it didn't matter anymore.

But this incident has stayed in my mind, a painful reminder of the way in which I eagerly seek forgiveness and mercy when it is my own need, but then reluctantly and hesitantly offer it to others. Jesus pulled no punches at the end of His story of the unmerciful servant. Describing the punishment meted by the angry king to the one who, though forgiven much, failed to forgive his brother, Jesus said, "This is how my heavenly Father will treat each of you unless you forgive your brother from you heart" (Matthew 18:35).

Willing to Forgive

That "from your heart" really makes it clear that forgiveness must be genuine and sincere—no burying of old bones to be dug up another day, but the complete eradication of the matter "from your heart." Easier said than done, you might be grumbling, as sometimes I have grumbled at God.

On the other hand, "from your heart" really sets us free to forgive. I have sometimes argued with God: "Look, I want to forgive her. I know I have to forgive her. But the memories are sharp and painful. I can't just forget."

And then I realize that, in forgiving, we lead with the heart. And if we forgive "from the heart," the head will come into line. It is in the heart that we effect a "letting go" of a grudge, a hurt, a painful experience. Only after that do we find that we can deal with the memories in an objective, open way.

I have moved from protest to rest simply by saying, "All right then. I am *willing* to forgive my friend. But that's as far as I can go. I have no power to forgive or to love. But I give the matter to You to deal with."

At such times I have a mental image of leaning over a bridge railing above a fast-flowing stream and tossing the matter over the edge, to be carried away by the swirl of the waters. And I discovered that, true to His faithfulness, God does the work of forgiveness through me—once I have willed to forgive in the matter. A wonderful principle of the Christian life had again proven true: "It is God who works in you to will and to act according to his good purpose" (Phillippians 2:13). And since forgiveness from the heart is always His good purpose, you can ask Him to give you the gift of forgiveness, and joyfully pass it on to another person. The thing that is impossible for you to do on your own becomes wonderfully possible with God's power at work in your life.

Some writers have suggested that our unforgiveness blocks God's blessing from another person's life. I don't know if that is so. But I do know that our unforgiveness makes it impossible for God to bless that person through us, as He might well desire to do. Unforgiveness clogs the arteries through which love flows. When we truly forgive "from the heart," we will to become God's channel of love and care to that person once again.

But if forgiveness is important for us to give, it is equally important for us to receive. And sometimes that is just as hard. It was for me. I was deadlocked in a personal conflict in which (as always!) I felt quite sure that I was right and the other party wrong. I remember standing by my kitchen sink, peeling potatoes with angry vigor while talking the matter over with a mature man of God. Suddenly I threw the peeler down and slammed the last freshly rinsed potato into the pot. "Look," I said, "I'm sick and tired of being forgiven for things I haven't even done."

He chuckled and then said firmly, with just a touch of Scottish burr softening the phrase, "But, Maxine, you will never know joy unless you can accept *that* forgiveness, too."

There it was: it was just as necessary for me to accept forgiveness that I felt was unwarranted as to offer forgiveness I felt was undeserved.

I gulped hard, and again could only say to the Lord, "O.K., Lord, I am willing to be forgiven."

Only after that was the Lord able to show me the way in which the other person felt, the slights and hurts that I had, however inadvertently, given her. And finally, although the process took some years, I was able to truly be grateful for her forgiveness and to accept it as the gift it was.

I am no expert on forgiveness. I only know that I can't live without it, that I need the forgiveness of God my Father too urgently to ever deny it to another person. I also know that I can't conjure forgiveness out of the air. It is a grace that God has to work in my life for each particular situation. I also know that any unforgiven matter in my life is like a poison in the spring of my ministry. It has to be dealt with. There simply are no options.

I remember a cold, bright January afternoon when Leona and I skied out across the pasture. Only the wind had been there before us, sculpting little dunes and frozen waves. We broke two trails, side by side, so we could talk through our frozen scarves.

"It just seems as though I have lost my communication with God," she said. "I can't go on like this any longer." A young businesswoman, she had once been a member of my teen Sunday school class. We skied up past the line of leafless poplars that crested the little rise in the pasture. "Can you put your finger on anything—any place or time where you began to lose touch with God?" I asked.

It was then that she began to spill her story. A friend had betrayed her, disappointed her, and finally rejected her. As we talked, we came to realize that unforgiven hurts, deeply held in her heart, had blocked her communication with the Father. In that strange inversion which is so often a feature of spiritual problems, the unforgiveness had lodged in the form of self-condemnation. "I don't blame her," she insisted. "I blame myself."

"Maybe," I commented, "that is just as bad. Forgiveness is the one gift you cannot afford *not* to give. It's a funny thing. Your unforgiveness may not hurt the other party in any way of which she is aware. But your unforgiveness will always hurt you." That afternoon I shared with Leona the important lesson I had learned about *willing* to forgive—or to be forgiven.

"It's a bit like the porcupine quills that Cam had to pull from our little Sheltie's nose last summer," I told her. I described how Butch had come sadly to the patio doors, his little pointed muzzle hung with a dozen hooked needles. I had watched while Cam, tenderly but firmly, removed each of the painful quills. As each quill came loose from the tender flesh, there was a little moan. But finally there was a dog who was free, bounding around, gratefully free of pain. "I guess the dog could have refused the hands of love that had to hurt to heal. But he would have suffered a greal deal more if he had."

Since Leona wanted to forgive—wanted to be in touch with God and with other people—I suggested a prayer exercise that I have learned over the years in struggling to learn how to forgive.

First of all, I suggested that she tell God that she was willing to forgive and let go whatever had hurt her. This turning of the will is a spiritual exercise, and the first step in coming into the sunlight of forgiving and being forgiven.

Secondly, I suggested that she draw up a list of people whom she felt had hurt her—a sort of forgiveness hit list. That list should become a daily prayer list, with each person on it prayed for by name. "Dear Father, I am naming 'X' before You. I forgive 'X' even as You, for Christ's sake, have forgiven me. Now I ask You to bless 'X' for Jesus' sake."

This is a special prayer exercise, and it releases joy and power in the life of the person who prays. I have found that I cannot ask God to bless a person more than two or three times before He has changed the attitude of my heart. In naming that person before God, the Creator and Redeemer, I begin to feel God's pulse of love for that person—and finally to share in its rhythm.

One of the gladdest moments of life comes after the exercise of the will, after the exercise of prayer, when fellowship is restored. And one day you find yourself wondering just what it was that you had found so hard to forgive. For forgiveness that starts in the heart finally reaches the head, too.

Extending Forgiveness

Just a word of caution may be in order here. All forgiveness does not have to be verbalized to the offending party. A person who is unaware of having wronged you might be rather amazed, and offended in turn, by your statement, "I want you to know I have forgiven you."

We are told to "set things right," to "deal with conflicts," to "confront in love." But there are lots of places in relationships for stillness and silence, and very often the matter of forgiveness is one of them. Only if the person who has wronged you is aware of his wrong and comes to seek forgiveness need anything be verbalized. And even then it can be a bit tricky. A dear old woman once came to a friend of ours and apologized for the way she had spoken to him the week before. Our friend could not remember any affront, but to put her mind at rest on the matter, he just gave her a little hug and said, "Your apology is accepted." Only later did he learn that she spent the next week mad at him for accepting her apology. "After all," she fumed to herself, "what I said wasn't *that* bad." Forgiving your friend or brother or enemy is basically a matter of the heart, a matter between you and God. It will be shown in the love you are able to share even with those who hate you—and that is far more important than mere words.

Welcoming the Brother Home

There is, of course, another kind of forgiveness: the corporate forgiveness of the Body of Christ for someone who has sinned, has confessed, and has been restored. Because we understand so little of church discipline, with its goal of restoration and reconciliation, we rarely experience the grace of corporate forgiveness.

One Sunday morning in our tiny village church we experienced one of those moments when the New Testament seemed to be open, with another chapter being lived. When Cam came to sit beside me after the choir had sung its anthem, he startled me with a scribbled note on the bottom of the day's bulletin: "John is here." John—back at church. A thrill ran through me, together with a moment of tension. Would he greet us? Would at last the long pain begin to subside?

John had come to our fellowship as a brand-new Christian. A Bible he had been given while hitchhiking across the continent had been the tool that God had used to bring him into new life. As he had read it, alone in his attic room back at home on the farm, the Spirit of God had revealed Jesus as Savior. John had received Him, and then had sought the fellowship of the developing little group of believers in the church. How we welcomed and loved him! His natural gift of music, now touched by the Spirit, was indeed a gift to the Body, and we rejoiced together in each new composition.

And then, in a sad and twisted parody of Christian love, a lonely young woman, separated from her husband, drew John into her life. We watched in anguish as, warnings brushed aside, the relationship quickly became a physical one. Finally we felt we had to ask John to resign his Sunday school class and step aside from public ministry in the church.

That had been over three years earlier, and he had left the church after a private, one-to-one conference, white with rage. He had gone on a three-day drinking binge, during which time he told anyone and everyone in our little community that he had been thrown out of the church. "They have done just what I thought they would do," he told his eager listeners. "They have crucified me."

The little flock of believers went through a baptism of fire. The community assaulted individuals with hostile criticism. What was essentially a church matter quickly became the talk of the pub, the club, the street corner. If a congregation's heart can break, then our collective heart broke. We cried and prayed together. We were without a minister at the time; we had nothing but the instructions of the Word of God to guide us. And to those we turned again and again. It was a matter of instrument-flying.

The woman involved moved away from our community, but it was for John we mourned.

One day as I sat at my friend Jeanne's to get my hair done, we were alone in her salon. "I believe he will come back" Jeanne said.

"Oh," I agreed, "I'm sure he'll come back to the Lord. But back to us?"

"Let's agree to ask God for that." And so we did.

But the time passed. We heard bits of news about John. While he had at first left our community to be with the young woman, that arrangement soon broke down and she left our part of the country. John was left, like a bit of flotsam on the beach, trying to sort out his life. Many months later had come good news: our new minister, a fine, true-to-the-Word preacher, had established contact with John.

And then, at last, the morning for which we had yearned and for which we had, against all hope, hoped: John was with us in morning worship.

The service continued according to plan. Our minister opened the Word to the appointed portion and began his sermon. "You know," he preached, "Elijah had confidence because he knew God's Word and delivered it to God's people. Sometimes that Word is a hard one to deliver. Sometimes that Word from God is one of rebuke. When a member of a congregation sins, and the church must, under the authority of God's Word, exercise 'tough love,' that is a hard Word." I felt myself drawing my breath in sharply.

"Don," I was crying in my heart, "what are you saying? Where are you going?" But Don was still speaking, and through the blur of pain I followed him.

"It isn't easy for a church to discipline a sinning brother. But when that brother repents, there comes a time for reconciliation and restoration, as we read in 2 Corinthians 2, verses 7 and 8:

'Now...you ought to forgive and comfort him so that he will not be overwhelmed by excessive sorrow. I urge you, therefore, to reaffirm your love for him.'

"Our brother John is here with us this morning," Don went on. "He phoned me yesterday and we spent a few hours together in preparation for today. He has asked if he might speak to you."

From the back row, John strode up to the platform. Blue-jeaned and blue-shirted, with a brown paper bag under his arm, he was followed by the loving eyes of the congregation. He faced us with composure, quiet tears shining in his eyes.

"I have come because I felt the Lord wanted me to come back to this place, to this congregation. I want to tell you that I am sorry for the shame I have brought on this congregation by my sin. I confess my sin which you all know about, and the much greater sin of anger and bitterness which I nursed in my heart for nearly three years. Some months ago I confessed my sin to the Lord, but I felt that I must confess to you as well and to ask you to forgive me. The blood of Jesus Christ has covered my sin. Now I ask to be restored to fellowship with you."

John pulled the brown bag from under his arm. "I brought some bread with me. It's some of my mom's bread, and you all know how good that is." It was the first time that we could smile together. "If you are willing to receive me as a brother, I invite you to come forward and accept a piece of this bread as a token of our renewed love."

The congregation moved out of the pews toward John, weeping with joy. And from his hands we received the bread that told of restoration and reconciliation. Together, we ate: a special communion, remembering the broken body of our Lord through which our broken Body had been healed. And then the service turned into celebration. "He is Lord," we sang, "His Name Is Wonderful," and "To God Be the Glory."

We stood together, reconciled, made one, whole again as a body. We knew we couldn't just go home to our separate houses. This was, if ever, an occasion for a love-feast. "Let's all come home to our place," Cam and I invited. "You bring what you can—and if you have nothing, come anyway." We hurried home to prepare. As the people came, the food came. What abundance! John had some turkey from a family gathering the previous day. I found cranberries. We cooked a huge pan of chili—and then came tins of ham and homemade buns and pickles and salads; and after that there were cakes and squares. We emptied and refilled the coffee urn and stirred up pitcher after pitcher of juice.

And then, after eating, with the children out playing soccer on the lawn, there was singing. John played his guitar while we sang together—all the loved songs we had set aside when he left us because they hurt too much—now sung together with a new joy.

Forgiveness is made possible by the forgiveness extended to us in Jesus Christ—forgiveness through which we "walk in the light as he is in the light" and "have fellowship with one another" (1 John 1:7). Each forgiveness is a healing—of the broken flow of God's love through us or to us. It is the one gift we need most, both to give and to receive.

9

The Gift of Time

It was a fall afternoon, gold with autumn coloring and bright September sun, when my good friend Deb came down from her lakeside home with her great big German Shepherd puppy, and a great big parcel for my birthday. Getting Deb and the gift into the house while keeping Juno out proved to be a challenge. I helped all I could by seizing the big box from under Deb's arm while Deb scooped Juno out the back door in one shiny tumble of black-and-tan fur.

Once safely upstairs, with Juno only occasionally making a sudden attempt at reentry through the patio screen, I set seriously about the task of opening the parcel. Inside, carefully packaged, was a beautiful clock set into a laminated still-life with copper kettle and glowing fruit and the reminder, "Enjoy the Blessings of This Day."

Deb turned the clock over and deftly installed the battery she had pulled from a jacket pocket. We turned the clock right side up—and laughed as we saw the second hand moving in tiny, dainty jerks—backwards!

It was the first time I had ever seen the seconds get counted *off* a clock. I could imagine watching the clock gradually taking me back through my life...to early wifehood...back to my teens...to the sunny, teary days of childhood...back to my own nothingness, and then back through time to the very beginning. It seemed a perfect gift for a woman who had just turned 40.

Deb found a switch at the back, and soon the slender, gold second hand began a more rational forward, clockwise, timewise motion that moved us forward toward eternity.

But often, when I glance at the clock, I have to quell a sudden chuckle at the surprise of backward-moving time, and remember that time does indeed run in only one direction: forward. The fact that we have just one life to live and that it is short is one with which we just reckon.

And that's what using the gift of time is all about. It is a gift given equally to all of us: 24 hours in every day we live. How we use it is up to us, but of course we will be accountable for it. Wasted hours, like idle words, will be answered for one day. Small wonder that the Apostle Paul encouraged the Ephesian believers to "be very careful, then, how you live—not as unwise but as wise, making the most of every opportunity" (Ephesians 5:15,16). Since time is a gift, it can be given and shared. One of the great joys of life is discovering that time can be exchanged for things other than money—that it can be given and received. I think of the hours of loving craftmanship that my friend Elsie gives me as she sews my wardrobe. I think of the hours that loving parents everywhere spend with their children—time given with no receipt asked for except love.

Time: Managed

We hear a lot about time management these days. I have even taught a seminar or two myself, although really I think I'm better at muddling through than at such sophisticated skills as time management. I have a few key principles by which I have learned to use my time, principles learned as a young mother with four small children—and a driving desire to write.

One of the first of those principles is the Principle of Planned Neglect. So, when someone asks me, "How ever do you do everything?" I find the answer easy: "I don't."

After a few years of playing the role of The Complete Country Wife, rolling out impossible pastry and punching down bread, it dawned on me that I was probably not making the best use of my time in terms of my abilities. So I traded in my pastry blender for a few minutes each day at my typewriter. Fortunately, I have a husband who thinks a finished manuscript is at least as great an accomplisment as an apple pie! In fact, he has taken the lead in showing me that lots of imagined needs, created by culture or by my own expectations, can be let go.

Some things can wait. Some things can be delegated. Some things can be done by machines. And some things do not need to be done at all. Like Martha serving supper, I can easily become "worried and upset about many things" when "only one thing is needed" (Luke 10:39-42). The one thing I can't neglect without damage to my entire life is time spent—however briefly—alone with the Lord. I need to clear a little space to spend alone with the Lord with my Bible open. Prayer is like a magnet held under a sheet covered with the random steel shavings which are the thousand concerns I have for that day. At the word of Christ, the shavings move into a beautiful radial pattern. The gift of time I make to Him becomes His gift of order and meaning to me as He who orders the universe brings order into each day.

Closely linked to the Principle of Planned Neglect is another time-handler I have learned to use. I call it the Principle of Purposeful Procrastination. It can be stated succinctly: "Never do anything today that doesn't have to be done today, but be sure to do everything that must be done today." When I am thinking through my day, I often list the activities that present themselves under three headings:

"Must Be Done," "Should Be Done," "Could Be Done." I do the "Must" jobs first, and let procrastination power keep me productive. Purposeful procrastination means an element of pressure in your schedule—and, like planned neglect, it requires a measure of self-discipline. But it can mean the difference between wishful thinking and productive living.

My final principle is one that has often helped me make the most of seemingly overfilled days, and has kept me from undue frustration when my accomplishments seemed few. It is the Principle of Ten Minutes At a Time. I learned about it first as a child from a bedtime story about a city bus driver who, at the end of his route, converted a plot of wasteland into a little park simply by using his ten-minute waiting time each day. And, in the press of family living and church commitments, I have learned that it is possible to move toward goals using ten minutes at a time.

Well, there you have it: Hancock's Three Principles of Time Management. Home-tested. Guaranteed to get you there. Of course, the decision as to where you want to get is yours to make. Obviously, if you are going to be able to give anyone the gift of your time, you need to husband your time effectively so that you have something to give.

The funny thing is that, the older I get and the longer I live, the less concerned I am about time management and the more aware I am of an even higher principle—that of time multiplication.

Time: Multiplied

Not long ago I sat at a brunch next to a beautiful woman, the wife of the minister of a large and clearly prospering church. She commented to me, in the course of our conversation, "You know, there is such a lot said abut how money given to God is multplied back to the giver. But few ever mention how time given to God is multiplied." I knew she was right.

The miracle of time multiplication has happened to me over and over again. I have learned over and over that time given to God and time given to other people is never lost. It is given back to me in increased effectiveness in many different ways.

It is a miracle that happens so often that I sometimes take it for granted. But the miracle of time multiplication took place unforgettably one clear winter morning. I had a major seminar coming up, and I had used my Principle of Purposeful Procrastination to push myself right up against the deadline in the preparation of my handouts for the course. I had, in fact, allotted myself exactly two days to get my course work prepared for presentation. I knew that if I worked steadily and with great intensity, I could get the job done in exactly that time—but not in a minute less. The materials were to be sent by courier to the seminar chairman so that they could be duplicated and ready for use.

I sat down with firm determination that morning and began to pound my typewriter and my head alternately, trying to bring ideas together. Finally the words and ideas began to flow. An hour into the morning, and my heart was singing. Everything was coming together. Thank You, Lord.

And then the phone rang.

A timid little voice at the other end said, "Maxine? I hope I didn't catch you when you were terribly busy."

"Why, not at all," I replied, sensing the urgency in the voice. "What can I do for you."

"Well—I've been trying to get up my courage to call you the past couple of months. I finally decided that today was the day. Can I come over and see you? There's something I need to talk with you about."

Of course. The voice was that of a new bride, a girl I had known through youth work several years earlier. I hung up the phone and ran up the stairs to put the coffee on. "Dear Lord," I whispered as I measured the coffee, "I am Yours. This work is Yours. This day is Yours. And if You want me to spend time with Wendy today, then I will need You to help me meet this deadline."

Back at the typewriter, I put in a productive half-hour

before the dogs barked to announce my visitor. Wendy and I sat down at the kitchen table. I had hardly poured the coffee into our mugs before she blurted out, "Well, I might as well get right to the point. I just had to come and see you because...well, because..." and suddenly her blue-blue eyes brimmed with tears, "because I can't live without Jesus any longer."

So I spent the morning helping her come back into His presence by confession of sin and renewal of the commitment that she had made when she first invited Him into her life. And I spent the afternoon rejoicing with her.

It was about 4:30 in the afternoon when I next sat down to the typewriter. But in the meanwhile, something had happened which had completely altered my situation. The phone had rung. This time it was the seminar chairman, wondering how I was doing with my preparation of material. Suddenly I heard her saying, "Look—why don't you just bring the materials along with you when you come. We'll duplicate them when you arrive."

It was a case of time multiplied by the same One who multiplied the little boy's loaves and fishes. How like the Lord! I had given Him just a few hours, and He had given me back a full week of preparation time. That is a kind of time multiplication that all the books on time management cannot tell you how to achieve. There is only one way: give time to the Lord; give time to others; and God can make the time you have left become double-time.

Not only have I found time sometimes extended, but I have also found it to be intensified. I sat down to outline messages for a conference recently. I had been thinking about the messages, praying about them, and dropping little notes into the file for them for several months. And I knew that, since it was a *Women Alive* conference, I was also being prayed for by a committed group of women. Having just finished my turn of full-time schoolteaching, I sat down to make outlines for the three messages at 11:45 one morning. "Please, Lord," I whispered. "A lot of women are going to gather—and they need to hear, not from me, but from You. Please share Your message with me."

I began to write, and when I was finished with the structural outlines for all three messages I felt jubilant, if drained. I glanced at the clock. It said 12:30. I blinked, unable to believe my eyes. "That clock must not be working," I thought, and wandered into another room to check that reading with another clock. Twelve-thirty it was! Only three-quarters of an hour had elapsed, and I had outlines for all three messages—a task I had thought would take me all day. Time in God's hands takes on some of the qualities of eternity.

It is from experiences like these that I have learned that while it is my job to manage my time, it is God's to multiply it. Time given to God in prayer or meditation and time given to other people in loving listening and serving is never time lost. It is truly time redeemed, and then wonderfully multiplied in effectiveness and power and given back into our hands.

On-the-Job Time

Quality time spent on the job should be one of the earmarks of Christians in the marketplace. The One who told us to "give to Caesar what is Caesar's" (Matthew 22:21) most assuredly requires that we give good time-value to our employers. Christians who arrive at half-mast because of deep-into-the-night discussions—even Biblical ones—are poor representatives of the Lord Jesus. Paul taught on this theme again and again, warning that believers should be "never...lacking in zeal" (Romans 12:11) in their daily work. The principle underlying Christian work-attitudes is most clearly stated in Colossians: "Whatever you do, whether in word or deed, do it all in the name of the Lord Jesus, giving thanks to God the Father through him" (Colossians 3:17).

The privilege of serving the Lord Christ is a genuine one, and should show up in the quality of every hour for which we claim pay. The worker who serves the Lord Christ does his work under the eye of that Master, and desires that in quality and in productivity there should be no cause for slander of the worthy name he bears.

In an office where I held a summer job, I once worked at a desk near another Christian girl. It was a large, bustling office, with high standards for worker output. But the girl across the desk from me was high on Jesus, high on meetings, and low on productivity. I winced at her attempts to witness to disgruntled fellow workers.

Because our daily work can be offered up as worship and service to our Lord, work well-done is just one of the many ways by which we do indeed redeem or buy up time. While we are exchanging our time for money in the marketplace, a necessary activity of life, we can add the extra value of conscientious, well-done work. Such was the distinctive of the early Christians. Such should be ours as well.

Once-Only Time

As my children go on growing up, I am constantly reminded that family time is "once-only time." I may have other chances to travel, to speak, to write, to teach, to study. But I will have this time, this once-only time, with these four children.

My sister-in-law, Barb, called a little word of admonition to me when her children were in their early teens, where mine are now. "If you think they take a lot of time when they're little," she said, "just wait until they're teens!" How right she has proved to be! They now need a different kind of time, a different quality of time, and time in a different part of the day. Now I feel as though the real work of my day begins at four o'clock or so—when the kids come home from school and unload—and continues until the last one is unwound and in bed, late in the evening.

In order to make the most of this "prime time," I have to discipline myself to adjust the work load of the earlier part of the day so that I am not strung out, too tired to interact with them.

Another kind of once-only time I am coming to value more and more is time with our parents. There will be a time when New Year's Day with Cam's parents or quiet evenings beside my parents' crackling fireplace will be only memories. One day they will all be with the Lord. But for now they are here with us, and time spent in making memories with them becomes more valuable with each passing year.

Other-People Time

Despite all that I have learned about the multiplication principle, I tend to want to be a time miser, to keep time for my own projects. My Lord goes on patiently teaching me that His first priority is people.

I learned something about making people a time priority one morning after my son Mitchell had gone to school. He had tried to show me how to make a cat's cradle. "Now take those two crossed strings," he had instructed, "and pull them under." We tried and tried again. "Aw," he said finally in disgust, "it won't work with this old knotted string."

In a few minutes the kitchen was quiet. I moved quickly to tidy counters and clear the table. Impatiently I gathered the knotted grocery string into a loose ball and walked to the garbage with it. As I started to toss it into the garbage bag, the Inner Voice said firmly, "Don't throw that away."

I talked back. "That's kind of silly. It's only worth a few cents. My time is too valuable to spend unknotting a piece of grocery string."

"It is? Who says?"

I walked back to the table, sitting down with the hopelessly knotted string. "Untie the knots now." The Voice was stern.

My stubborn, impatient, blunt fingers began to work, struggling to untie each stubborn knot. To my surprise, the knots yielded to me, one after another. As I worked, I carried on a silent dialogue with the Voice.

"This really is nonsense," I fumed at first, scratching with my fingernails to get a grip on a tiny, tight knot. "You know I haven't time for this."

"I know."

"And You know," I went on, "that I haven't patience for this."

"I know."

"Then why are You asking me to do it?"

"Because there is something I want to teach you today."

"I'm listening, Lord," I sighed, as I carefully smoothed the first straightened string into a carefully folded hank, neat and ready to use. I picked up the next length of string and began unknotting it as the Inner Voice talked quietly to me.

"The reason you think you don't have time is that you have accepted the world's formula that time equals money. It does for the world. But in my economy, time can equal something far more lasting than money. Time can equal eternity: the eternity of a human soul. Time spent with people, time spent with me, is time which is translated into eternal time."

"Is that what You mean, Lord, in the phrase 'redeeming the time'?"

"That's it. I mean for you to buy time back from the world's money-based economy and use it for eternal investment."

"I think I follow that, Lord. But now, what about untying knots? It's hard, Lord, and I'm not a patient person. Why does it matter that I do this right now? I had other things planned. What's so important about this silly old string?"

"I want you to see that the string is important just because it *exists*. It's so much easier to destroy than it is to create. But I'm not just teaching you about string."

"I know, Lord," I whispered. And I thought about people—people whose lives are so knotted up that the world finds it easier to throw them away than to work to untie the knots, to set them free for life. I was thinking about Chris, a European woman who had come to live with our family, drug-damaged and bitter about the futility of life. She met our Lord, and life began to have meaning. I thought, too, about Kitty, the girl who decided she could stay with us and finish her year of school. She was now holding a steady job and was involved in a church fellowship in a distant city. I thought of Karin, my frightened and loveless young neighbor, who had sat and watched me bake bread and tend my children and had finally stopped railing against God long enough to hear Him out—and had found that He was love. By now tears were blurring my work with the third hand of string. "This is Your task," the Lord was saying quietly.

"Why me? I am the most impatient person in the world."

"That's why. Because you are unable, and the ability will have to come always from me. My heart is with the throwaways, the knotted strings, the people whom I have created but whose lives have become a tangled mess. I asked you to unknot these little pieces of grocery string to show you that. If you can understand that string is important to me, you might be able to catch a glimmer of how important people are to me."

The three strings lay folded and without knots on the table beside my Bible. I picked up the Book and read the passage to which I had been directed earlier that morning: "I will seek that which was lost, and bring again that which was driven away, and will bind up that which was broken, and will strengthen that which was sick" (Ezekiel 34:16 KJV).

And all I could say was, "Yes, Lord. Bring us the knotted strings."

I put the strings in the drawer under the telephone, ready for the next attempt at cat's cradle.

"Let me help you untie lives and make them ready to be Christ's cradle," the Spirit whispered. And, with a new sense of purpose and calling, I went about my work.

Only One Lifetime

Psychologists have described the "midlife crisis" in which we struggle to accept our own mortality. The runaway bestseller *Passages*, by Gail Sheehy (E.P. Dutton, 1976), made us all aware of this. As Christians, we know that mortality is only the gateway to immortality, and so one would expect that crisis to be somewhat muted for us.

In practice, however, the Christian may find that the midpoint in life makes him even more acutely anxious than it does his unbelieving neighbor. For he has a vision of time that can have eternal significance. How can he best order the second half of his life to reflect that understanding? He wrestles with choices and cries with the psalmist, "Teach us to number our days aright, that we may gain a heart of wisdom" (Psalm 90:12).

I was sharing with a professional colleague of mine the dilemma which Cam and I faced: each of us had a well-developed teaching career, but each of us also had a hobby that had grown like Topsy. The farm was now a major enterprise; my writing had developed into a career of its own. "Yes," she nodded sympathetically, "one has to choose what one's life-thrust is to be."

That's it, I thought. That's it exactly. Life-thrust— direction—the priority by which one sets all other priorities. As I have reflected on that comment in the light of acutely difficult midlife choices, I suddenly realize that our life-thrust cannot be teaching or farming or writing. Our life-thrust has to be in terms of our relationship to God and to other people. Paul summed it up this way: "For to me, to live is Christ and to die is gain" (Philippians 1:21). My days in InterVarsity Christian Fellowship gave me its motto as mine: "To know Christ, and to make Him known."

That is the life-thrust that makes sense of these little lives; that is the life-thrust that helps us sort out time and commitment. It is in the light of such a life-thrust that we husband the gift of time—and gladly share it with others for whom Christ died.

Part Three

The Motive and the Manner

Christian giving springs from a
different headwater from all other
kinds of giving. It is motivated by
gratitude and issues in grace.

10

Giving and Receiving Gracefully

"Audrey," I said, looking across the farm kitchen table at my sister-in-law, "what a lovely pin you have on your jacket!"

"Do you like it?" she smiled.

"I really do," I said, looking at it just a little closer. "It has such a lovely, fine design."

Audrey's smile broke into a little chuckle. "Glad you like it," she said. "You should. You gave it to me last Christmas!"

It was not an especially graceful moment in my experience of giving. But the gale of laughter we shared made it one of the more memorable ones. Really, when I talk about doing anything gracefully, I have to be just a little bit tongue-in-cheek. Just over five feet tall, I have never been offered a modeling contract. Never. Recently I stood with a friend at a conference. Scanning the milling coffee-break crowd, he commented, "I see a lot of unfamiliar faces."

"Oh, really," I said. "How nice. I see a lot of unfamiliar elbows."

I do not, like a model friend of mine, "come on tall." Nor, most of the time, do I "come on graceful."

But what I really care about, more than about poise or personal grace, is to learn to live, and give, and receive in a way that is truly grace-filled, truly motivated by grace. I have a deep and growing desire to be, as Jesus was, "full of grace and truth" (John 1:14). I have received so much of His grace: common grace extended through family and friends and beautiful hoar-frosted mornings and deep-dyed sunsets, and special grace in conscious awareness of His presence in my life as Lord and Savior. I want to live in that grace, and be not only a grace-receiver but also, to those around me, a grace-giver. I want, with God's help, to live gracefully.

I think giving gracefully, like all charity, must begin at home. I pondered one day a harsh interchange I had heard between my children, recognizing with grief the echo of my own strident tones. And I realize that I, a child of grace, was a mother of law, and that my children were learning from me not grace but law. I ached—and asked— that I might learn how to extend grace to my children by unconditional, no-strings-attached love, by demonstrating to them that their acceptance as persons is independent of performance. As I pursued the idea of becoming a grace-giver to my children, I learned that *forebearing* was as important a principle as *forbidding*. I learned to give forgiveness in a new and freeing way: unconditionally, forgettingly. And I learned, too, to accept that kind of forgiveness from my children.

Grace-filled giving and receiving means building our personal relationships on the same basis as our relationship with God. It begins with living in the confidence that we are accepted by God for reasons which arise entirely from His heart of love, and not at all from our loveliness. And then it becomes our privilege to extend that kind of grace and acceptance to all who enter our homes or our lives.

Giving and Receiving As Gratitude

Giving that is truly Christian springs from a different headwater from all other kinds of human giving. Christian giving stems from our response to God's love and grace. It is "gratitude giving." It springs first and always from a sense of wondering gratitude for God's gifts so generously given.

Only the child of God who has experienced the grace of God in salvation can truly understand how the desire to give to others wells up from the awareness of "amazing grace." In gratitude for the love of God given to us in the Person of His Son, the Christian seeks channels through which the free flow of glad giving can find its way to meet the needs of others.

Other Motivations

This does not mean that we do not face the problem of motivation. All around us, expecially in church circles, are subtle appeals to other kinds of motivation. There is the appeal *to give in order to get*: "Give and you will be sure to be blessed," we are urged. We are also told that the blessing is likely to be in kind: if we give lots of money we will be sure to get lots of money. It is a base and debasing reason for giving, but it is one which preys subconsciously on desires that are part of our inherent human selfishness. Repeatedly in the New Testament, "covetousness" or the desire for things is listed along with sins that we would all consider ugly (see Romans 1:28-32 and Galatians 5:19-21, for example). And yet, pathetically enough, in our Christian circles today we attempt to launder covetousness and make it somehow an acceptable motivation for giving.

It just won't wash.

A step up the motivational ladder from giving to get is the motivational invitation: *"It feels good to do good."* Of course it does. But that is not the reason for giving—at least not for Christian giving. It is a well-nigh universal experience that there is a tremendous joy in giving—enhanced, of course, if our gift is recognized, received with thanks, and responded to with proper gratitude.

But to give "because it feels good" limits our giving to the kind that does indeed feed back ego-strokes. Yet there is important giving to be done that does not feel particularly good. There is giving that hurts. And if our only motivation is hedonistic, we will not undertake that kind of giving. I am sure that very often Mother Teresa's giving does not feel—or smell— particularly good. She has to draw on deeper motivation to carry on her work among the dying and forgotten. That deeper source is an awareness of God's giving which reaches out, through the deepest kind of suffering, to the most ungrateful of His creatures.

Furthermore, giving "because it feels good" has its here-and-now reward, and thus robs us of any further, eternal dimension to our giving. "Surely," Jesus said about the public, self-congratulatory giving of the Pharisees, "they have received their reward in full" (Matthew 6:2).

Another motivation is that *giving is a survival tactic*. Increasingly, modern writers are pointing out that giving is a good way of looking out for yourself. "Altruistic egoism" is how stress-investigator Hans Selye defines his philosophy. He states it simply—"Earn thy neighbor's love."[1] This philosophy says that it is less stressful for me to live companionably with my neighbor, since, as I do him a good turn, he is sure to do me one. And again, as all neighborly souls know, that is certainly true. However, this is not a reason to give but rather a natural consequence of normal, neighborly giving.

A more desperate form of egoistic giving is described in Terence des Pres's study *The Survivor* (New York: Oxford, 1976). Des Pres points out that survivors of extermination camps were those who learned how to give favors in exchange for advantage within the prison camps, and thus put themselves in the best position to survive.

Perhaps the clearest visual picture I carry of the difference between giving in order to survive and giving out of gratitude for Christ's self-giving comes from the film version of *The Hiding Place*. The tough-as-nails nurse who knows how to use the prison system to her own advantage illustrates "the survivor" as portrayed by des Pres. But Corrie Ten Boom is another kind of survivor—one who gives to others not to gain advantage but simply because giving is true to her nature as a child of God.

Christian giving is not even motivated by the highest of purely natural human motivations: *response to human need.* Altruistic giving surely represents the highest level of human interaction. We thrill to selflessness wherever we find it, whether in the pages of history or the pages of *Time*. But Christian giving is different even from this, for it is occasioned not by a specific need but by a general gratitude. However that gratitude focuses itself, whatever needs it meets, its primary direction is Godward. "We love because He first loved us" (1 John 4:19).

This matter of motivation can cause us a lot of pain. We find ourselves concurring with Jeremiah's statement, "the heart is deceitful above all things" (Jeremiah 17:9). We find that, even when we have examined our hearts, our motivation is often double, dimly lit, deeply hidden. What do we do about it? Do we withhold our gifts until we are certain our motivation is right?

I struggled in anguish of spirit over this when I first began to write. For me, writing was my way of giving, of sharing from my life. I felt that I must write—or explode. And yet my motivation was quite unclear. Was I giving to get?

Writing to make money? The Lord knows how much those little checks meant to me. When first they began to arrive they were, in those far-off, hard-pressed days, often like gifts straight from heaven. One check especially I remember. I was writing and sending out articles, but I needed more background, especially in marketing. And then one day I saw an article in *The Edmonton Journal* describing an authors' convention to be held in Edmonton. Quickly I phoned the contact number. Yes, nonmembers were welcome. Even those who were just beginning to write? Most assuredly.

I hung up the phone. The only thing that stood between me and the conference was the $20 registration fee and the two days of baby-sitting that I would have to pay for. This was money that just didn't appear in our bare-bones budget. "Lord," I prayed, "if this is something I should get to, please send me a check from my writing to confirm it." In hope, I made arrangements for a high school girl to come with me to the city for the two days. In hope, just a day or two before the conference, I received a check—for my first real article accepted by *Moody Monthly*. I can still see the rosy hue of that pink check for the lordly sum of $50—exactly what I needed for registration and baby-sitter. I loaded my little ones and their baby-sitter into the car and headed for the city.

But was it really those small earnings that I was writing for? Or was it something even more subtle—a desire to be known? The Lord knows how much any writer enjoys his name and his ideas in print. Printer's ink is both intoxicating and at least mildly addictive. I wrestled with the problem for days. Was I just an exhibitionist? The fact was that I couldn't really find the reason for my inner urgency to write—an urgency that drove me to find a half-hour to write each day even when I had two children under two years of age.

Finally I knelt down with my notebook open and poured out the whole confusion of my heart to God.

> O Lord God:
> You know my heart.
> Can You do anything with me?
> Can I write—and please You?
>
> I believe that I must simply cease to try
> To sort out all the motives, deeply hidden,
> And just obey.
> You have said "Give,"
> And so I'll give,
> And as I do

The purifying fire of Your Holy Presence,
the fire from off the altar,
the burning coal,
may scorch my lips and burn out what defiles.
Amen.

I got up from my knees, free in a new way—free to write
and to leave the motivation to God. Now I have a mental
picture of what the Lord does for us when we decide to obey,
to give, even while we are not sure of how pure our motivation may be.

I remember how we used to have to light the Bunsen
burners in the chem lab in order to do our high school
chemistry experiments. I remember that initial "poof" and
the up-leaping flame, smoky and yellow, that made us jump
back. And then we would adjust the gas and the oxygen
valves, clarifying the flame. At last we would get a pure blue,
silent flame which neither called attention to itself nor
demanded special attention, but drawing on its hidden
source, burned with a clear, bright heat.

And so it is with all forms of giving. Recognizing that giving begins with receiving, we move forward in obedience.
We resist the desire to introspect and to analyze, for that
leads only to confusion and self-disgust. We simply give
ourselves—our total motivational system—into the hands
of the One who can search and purify our hearts. And then
we go ahead and give: gracefully, gratefully.

Jacob in the Old Testament shows us the way. His deal-
ings with God are marked at first by unmitigated selfishness.
He makes a business deal with God—and amazingly, God
honors it. Jacob gives to get. But as the years pass, and he
walks on through life, God brings into his life circumstances
that change that man. And one night he has a radical, total
encounter with a God who is Lord, and the old cheater
becomes a Prince with God.

And so we, who are receivers of grace, give. We give
whatever is in our power to give. We ask God, by His Spirit,

to purify our motives until one day we will burn with a clear, silent, upward-pointing flame of love "to him who loves us and has freed us from our sins by his blood, and has made us to be a kingdom and priests to serve his God and Father— to him be glory and power for ever and ever! Amen" (Revelation 1:5,6).

11

No Obligation But Love

I have a daughter who loves to give. As Christmas or a birthday draws near, her eyes shine with untold secrets and scarcely-containable surprises. The sheer joy of finding "just the right thing" for a special person fills her with exultation. "I love it, I love it!" she exclaims as she spreads out her carefully chosen gifts on her bed for my inspection. "Just look at this! Do you think Dad will like it? Oh, I hope so!" Her delight serves as a model to me of the way in which giving should be done. Generously. Gladly. Graciously.

Dour, obligatory giving; resentful, sulky receiving; stinginess or prideful rejection of gifts: all are equally ungraceful, equally foreign to the spirit of giving in love.

As those who "know the grace of our Lord Jesus Christ, that though he was rich, yet for [our] sakes he became poor" (2 Corinthians 8:9), we just cannot help but give. And we give with joy. The sound of holy laughter should echo around every gift we give. For it is in moments of giving and self-forgetfulness that we are sprung loose from the grip of anxious concern. We become like little children—enthralled in the simple, sweet joy of making someone else happy or of meeting a need. And that freedom resonates with the song of the spheres and echoes through eternity.

Give and Receive With Joy

"Each man should give what he has decided in his heart to give, not reluctantly or under compulsion, for God loves a cheerful giver" (2 Corinthians 9:7). As we have already seen, it is the abounding grace of God that makes giving possible at all. The response of the heart to that grace can only be joy-filled giving. The person who, with the psalmist, discovers that God's mercies are new every morning is one who is prepared to give—and receive—with growing joy.

I give with great joy because I have received with great joy. I love to think about some of the things I have received. With Christmas just past, I think of the ruffled flannelette nightie that one daughter sewed for me, and the cosy pink housecoat that the other children "went together" for. But it is not "thing gifts" which stand out most in my mind. It is the time that Heather Ruth first invited me to listen to her read *Wind in the Willows*. It is the moment of insight that Mitchell shares in one of his frequent philosophic moments. It is Cammie-Lou's early morning music, floating up to my room before dawn on these dark northern winter mornings. It is the sureness of sonship that Geoffrey demonstrates—and invites me to recognize in my relationship with God. It is Cam's smile.

It is the touch of my mother's hands, smooth and cool and dry as parchment. It is the resonance of my father's voice, lifted in prayer, with phrases balancing against each other and words rung like bells.

It is the remembrance of teachers who corrected and encouraged me. Of Miss Margaret Molloy, who introduced me to *A Book of Good Essays* and the magic of the great English stylists. Of Miss Agnes Lynass, who introduced me to *Hamlet* and the glorious diversity of English literature.

It is the remembrance of friends who have held me in their hearts and in their arms. It is the lamplight in my hotel room, last month when Lorrie White, wife of writer Dr. John White, sat with me after the final meeting of an exhausting conference, and ministered her love and gracious presence to me, sharing her quiet wisdom and insight.

Such tokens of love I hold in my mind like a handful of smooth stones to hold, to look at, to touch again. And each of us has such treasures. The trick is to remember. And then, realizing how richly we have received, we become glad givers. It is our joy, our delight, to give as we receive.

Give and Forget

Like all forms of art, giving includes "the art that conceals art." Just as the great artist makes his work appear to be the inevitable way of expressing the idea it contains, hiding the months of struggle with technique and design behind a natural simplicity, so the giver who has truly learned the art of giving from the Great Giver knows how to conceal the struggle and growth behind the giving, and make each gift exactly the natural thing to do under the circumstances. When Jesus warned us not to perform our charity in the marketplace "before men, to be seen by them" (Matthew 6:1), He was teaching us something about the art that conceals art: giving quietly and unobtrusively.

The simple practice of removing a price tag before giving a gift is an expression of the necessity of concealment of the cost. (Who has not shared with me the painful embarrassment of waiting to lay hands on a gift in order to peel a forgotten price tag off the bottom? It's worse, of course, if the price tag is one of those vivid markdown stickers!)

Often, Christian giving requires that not only the cost of the gift but even the giver himself should be hidden. If we are to know the reward of the Father in heaven, Jesus taught, we must not collect our little private rewards here. Names engraved on plaques and elaborate expressions of gratitude may satisfy our egos, but they may also rob us of the greater reward: the "well done" for which we yearn. In every giver's repertoire of giving there should be some secrets— some gifts given in such a way that the recipient has no one to thank but the Father.

The giver who has truly learned the art of giving knows how to "give it and forget it." He does not keep a catalog of his gifts, nor does he keep a corresponding list of obligations. He does not even keep a checklist to see what repayment has been made or what gratitude has been expressed. These are foreign to the spirit of Christian giving. He makes the gift, and whether it is gracefully received or not, he simply lets it go. There are no strings attached, no implied I.O.U's. It is just a gift, freely and simply given, and filled with grace.

Receive and Remember

This same simplicity and clarity should mark the Christian as he receives a gift from another person. There need be no obsequiousness, no fawning—just a shared moment of gratitude, a clearly expressed and deeply meant "Thank you."

I had always taken this grace-receiving for granted until, after we married, we made some friends who gave in another way. I was at first overwhelmed by their kindness, then puzzled by their sudden flare-ups or cool-downs. Finally I caught on. Every kindness they did was, in their minds, a kind of demand note, to be called at their pleasure and repaid on their terms.

Needless to say, we became very cautious about letting them do anything for us, since the only way we could preserve our autonomy was to refuse to be in their debt.

It was a painful lesson, but it showed me the glory and joy of truly Christian giving—giving that imposes no obligation but love.

Of course, a spirit of gratitude should mark God's people so that even small kindnesses are noticed and genuine appreciation is expressed between brothers and sisters. Taking the gifts of other people for granted is no more Christian than publishing the names of donors. "Do nothing out of selfish ambition or vain conceit, but in humility consider others better than yourselves" (Philippians 2:3). That is best done through an attitude of awareness and appreciation for the many ways that God's gifts are given to us through others.

And while a gift given can be forgotten, a gift received is a delight to remember, something to cherish, something to give thanks for in many ways. One day while I was shopping I suddenly remembered a friend who had looked after one of our children while I was in the hospital. At the time I had thanked her, but I had had no other way to acknowledge her kindness. But on that day, several years later, I saw a small gift I could give her as a love-token, something that would tell her that her love and kindness were remembered. What fun it was to purchase that little gift, to wrap it up and surprise her with it! What fun to reminisce together about the times we had shared when neither of us had anything but our love and time to give to each other!

Giving with Grace

The nature of a true gift is that it is a little bit of grace—something given freely, not as payment and certainly not for repayment. It is something given on the basis of the need of the receiver and the resources of the giver.

I remember reflecting on this once when a little gift I had joyfully given was deflected. I had visited with a woman who commented that she loved the poems of Robert Frost.

Later, strolling in a bookstore, I saw an edition of Frost's poems, and on a whim I bought them for her. Only a few days later, a wrapped gift arrived at my door—a china cup and saucer with a thank-you note. I had the distinct feeling that, rather than seeing the book as a gift, my neighbor had seen it as an obligation, and one to be repaid as quickly as possible.

Giving that is not gracious—that is, which does not begin and end in grace—often becomes a kind of power game. One of the really unattractive aspects of extended family in the rural setting is the way in which parents, sometimes grown wealthy over the years, maintain effective control over the lives of their children deep into adult life simply by giving or withholding gifts. There is nothing more pathetic than to watch sons and daughters attempt to out-bedside each other as they await the passing of a parent who has held them in serfdom since childhood.

This is not the giving of grace, but the wielding of power. Gracious giving responds to need and invites only the response of gratitude. Gracious giving always preserves the personhood of the receiver, granting him full autonomy.

Gracious giving lacks the condescension that makes some gifts so hard to receive. It does not draw distinctions: "I have, and you have not." It recognizes that we are all both "haves" and "have-nots." Every one of us has something to share and something we need. Gracious giving is always mutual, recognizing our need to receive as well as give.

Receiving with Graciousness

Gracious receiving is an art, too. It goes beyond appreciation for the gift to acknowledging the worth of the giver. The gift is the token of the giver, and true gratitude is not just for the gift but also for the person who shared himself through the gift. Teaching children to write thank-you notes is one of the more thankless tasks of parenting—and one of the more important. I can remember how, after Christmas wrappings were gathered, my brother and sisters and I would be gathered around the dining-room table, pens in hand, to write thank-you notes to grandparents and aunts and uncles.

I was about nine when I wrote to my grandmother, "I can scarcely thank you sufficiently for the exquisite doll you selected for me." On I went, exploiting my growing vocabulary to the full, until my mother read my note over my shoulder.

"Oh dear," she said, "just be simple. Tell your grandmother that you like the doll. That's enough."

And so I learned that receiving, like giving, should be with simplicity. And sincerity. Better a short, sincere thank you than an ostentatious, formal note which amounts to little more than acquiescence to social form. The breezy, bright note I received just the other day—"Very, very nice. That's how Betsy describes the covered casserole..."—made me feel glad I had taken the time to choose something special for that couple.

I remember one night when our village church choir gathered after our regular practice to say farewell to one of our members. Since the young woman had very little money, the choir had taken up a generous collection and had purchased a set of luggage for her travels. Overcome at the gift, the young woman whispered to me, "But it's far more than I deserve."

I found myself whispering back, "Of course. It has nothing at all to do with what you deserve. It has everything to do with how you are loved."

How Shall We Give? How Receive?

Let us give and receive *humbly*, acknowledging our need of others and the gifts that they give us, even as we see their needs and bring to them our glad gifts.

Let us give and receive *openhandedly*, acknowledging that others bring to us gifts from the very heart of the Father, even as we give our gifts from the same gracious Source.

Let us give and receive *simply*, accepting and giving each

gift for what it is: a gift, but not an obligation to anything but love; a gift, but not a means of subtle control through implied obligation.

Let us give and receive *freely*, receiving without grasping, giving without demanding repayment.

The cycle of giving begins with receiving and goes on in an endless reciprocation of giving and receiving and giving again. Perhaps it is because we must all be both givers and receivers that the Lord has given each of us two hands. Should one hand—either the giving or receiving one—be at first cramped and twisted, as we reach out it will be strengthened, shaped by the gift, healed. In Jesus' healing and restoration, each of us can learn to be both a giver and a receiver.

12

Giving and Receiving As Ritual

My friend Karen has a strong sense of ritual—small, personal ritual. When we were in high school we had a weekly rite of stopping for Danish pastry at a bakery near our school. And when, a little while ago, I was able to spend a couple of days with her in California, she taught me some more about the rituals of giving and receiving.

"But you have just got to take something home to the kids," she told me.

"I don't usually," I shrugged. (I travel light, especially when it comes to cash. And since I am usually short of time and luggage space, too, gift-getting is normally out of the question.) "I've never made a habit of taking anything home."

"Well, then, you should start now. We'll go shopping this morning."

In and out of little gift shops along Malibu Beach she took

me. We laughed over cards and looked at possibilities. There were shells and dolls and trinkets and plush toys. But everything was too expensive or not just right. "Look, Karen," I said, "let's not use up our whole visit shopping. The kids won't really be expecting anything."

"Well, then, that's all the more reason why they should have something. There's one more mall I want to take you to. It has a special toy shop." Again we got into her station wagon. Again I looked, rather halfheartedly, at a selection of gift items which by now were all looking rather familiar.

"Wouldn't this be nice for Mitchell?" she asked, showing me a puppet.

I shook my head. "I don't think he'd really care for it."

But Karen was patient and persistent. "How about a yo-yo?"

"He's got two already."

"O.K.," she said firmly. "Let's just walk around the corner and check out this store at the corner. And then we'll quit. I promise."

And that's where she showed me translucent, delicately tinted acrylic boxes: tiny boxes of many shapes and sizes, each with a perfectly fitting lid. Finally I was excited. "Look, Karen. I could buy one of these boxes for each of the children, and then put tiny things into them."

She shared my joy. "I thought you might like those," she said. We bought the boxes for a few cents each and then started back though the gift shops in reverse order, choosing some small trinket or sea shell for each child, something just the right size to put into one of the boxes.

What joy it was to carry those tiny gifts home to my children! For Geoff, a red acrylic box filled with fine sand from Malibu Beach. For Mitchell, a delicate sea-horse skeleton in a pale-blue box. For Cammie-Lou and Heather Ruth, abalone-shell necklaces in mauve-and-pink boxes. The total cost—under five dollars. But the ritual of selection, of carrying home and presenting, made the gifts of value far beyond the things-in-themselves.

Ritual Giving

The rituals of giving and receiving are deeply embedded within the context of any culture. Children learn the rituals early. I remember how a toddler would initiate a "let's pretend" game. Round hand tightly closed around an invisible treasure, one of the children would come to me. "Would you like some candy?"

"Why, yes, please, I would," I would reply, obediently filling in the unstated formula that governed the game.

"Here you are," she would say, laying the little fist into my open hand. She would unclench her hand then, and the invisible "gift" would pass from her hand to mine.

"Thank you very much," I would say, and savor the imagined sweet, together with the very real sweetness of the game. Of course the game was not about candy; it was about the ritual of giving and receiving. In a society which shares very few universal rituals any longer, the rituals of giving and receiving are still well-understood and widely observed.

What are the essentials of ritual giving? There is the request or expectation of a gift befitting a particular occasion, the selection and presentation of that gift, and finally the rituals of acceptance: appropriate expressions of appreciation. These are firmly structured and solidly grounded in our culture. The particular occasions for ritual giving may differ from family to family, but the generalized "formula giving" is similar.

Spontaneity and Ritual

Being a spontaneous person, I have been slow to understand the meaning and worth of ritual giving—or of ritual anything, for that matter. I could understand the joy of giving and the meaning of gifts, but I found it hard to acquiesce to the idea of gifts-on-demand or of mandatory giving. I guess I felt most keenly about wedding gifts. I could understand how, years ago, when a couple set out to start a new home, the ritual of wedding gifts expressed community support for the development of a new home and family unit. I was less able to see why young people in our day should be assisted by more or less mandatory gifts to begin life at a higher standard of living than what many of their parents had yet achieved.

However, the longer I live, the greater is my respect for institution and tradition, for rituals which bind people to each other and the present to the past. At a time when the fragile web of human society seems in danger of being torn apart through carelessness and neglect, the affirmation of solidarity and caring through ritual gift-giving is worthy of our attention.

I have been aided in my pilgrimage toward understanding the value of ritual by being married to an antiformalist. For Cam, the essence of life is spontaneity. "Who is to tell me that this is Mother's Day, and that therefore I am to express my appreciation to you?" he has said indignantly. "I love and appreciate you every day." And it is true. He does. Why, then, do I feel just a little bit blue when special days and occasions slip by unmarked? Something in me must cry out for the ritual of gift-giving, even when I am deeply reassured that the essence behind all gifts is surely mine.

And why, despite our avowed distaste for *formal* gift-giving, should the gifts that stand out in my mind be those which were given ritualistically? Most special of those memories is of a golden September harvest day when Cam left a telephone message at the school for me to stop by at the field where he was combining wheat. Thinking he probably needed me to drive to the next town for parts, I wearily went to the field. Cam stopped the combine and ran, jumping across swaths as he came. Taking a small box from his khaki workshirt pocket, he handed it to me. "Happy birthday, Darling. I love you." The lovely little pendant in the box is my favorite piece of jewelry, and probably always will be. The context, of being specially remembered on a special day, enhances it far beyond any "book value" it may have.

And so, far from being an antiformalist (as I once thought myself to be), I have come to recognize the importance of rituals in relationship to giving and receiving.

The danger, of course, is that ritual giving becomes a purely commercial activity. A gift that is ritually requested by a wedding invitation or by the repeated reminder "Do you know when my birthday is?" is in danger of becoming a chore, a duty, an obligation—rather than a celebration of the opportunity to affirm the person to whom we give.

Ritual giving, like all our giving, should be marked by joy. The gifts should be given as a way of celebrating life and the privilege of living and loving in human community. The simple interchange of gift given and formally acknowledged is a bond, however tenuous, between persons. All such bonds should be cherished.

Probably we can best minimize the danger of purely commercial giving by remembering that gifts are at best tokens or symbols. It is not the gift as thing-in-itself which is of the greatest importance, but rather the gift as symbol-of-love.

The first question we should ask about a gift is not "How much should I spend?" but "What do I want this gift to say?" Ritual giving takes on a different texture when it is approached this way—a more human kind of nubbiness.

Wedding Gifts

Wedding gifts chosen in this way can symbolize our love for the young people being married and our esteem for the "holy estate of matrimony." Things which reflect the essentials of a home—bowls and sheets and towels—are probably better than luxury gadgets, all too soon obsolete or in need of repair. Items which are beautiful in design can reflect our awareness of the gracious pattern of marriage. Those which combine usefulness and beauty of love is shown in daily duties. Craftspeople, of course, have a special advantage in being able to make gifts of enduring and personalized beauty. For me, a homemade patchwork quilt has been especially loved, a constant reminder of a special friend.

And let's not overlook the gifts that will serve as reminders that "Christ is the sure Foundation, Christ the Head and Cornerstone." For many years we have given padded editions of a Bible to young couples, each inscribed with a personal note sharing the way in which we have found the Word of God to be the source book for the kind of love that is needed in a marriage. Beautiful, contemporary Scripture plaques are a joy to give, too. I would like to hang the text "Jesus is Lord" in every new Christian home in the country—in some spot where it has to be reckoned with in conversation, confrontation, and decision-making.

Birthday Gifts

Birthdays are another occasion when ritual giving is called for in our society. Especially in a home where a child shares his parents' attention with several siblings, birthdays serve the very important function of drawing special, loving attention to one particular child for that particular day. Birthdays provide an opportunity to celebrate the child—his interests, his stage of development.

But birthdays are not only for children; birthdays also provide an opportunity to affirm our love for our spouses or for aging parents or friends. They present an opportunity for us to repudiate the world's infatuation with youth. Some very special things only become more valuable with time, including rare books and fine china. And so it is with life's deepest relationships.

Christmas Gifts

Besides weddings and birthdays, the other major occasion of ritual giving sanctioned by our society is Christmas. It presents a special dilemma to Christians: how do we maintain the meaningful giving and receiving of gifts without bowing the knee to the golden cow of commercialism? How do we prevent Christmas giving from becoming a matter of dumping a prescribed number of dollars by a defined deadline?

Simply to be sour about "commercialism" is not the answer. I realized this one day when a European girl working for us told me flatly, "I think Christmas should be abolished. It means nothing to me. The religious aspect has no meaning at all for me. And the gift-giving is nothing but a bother." Since she was the most totally self-engrossed young person I had ever known, I could see why the gift-giving would be a problem to her. But I suddenly knew that for me it should not be.

Christmas giving becomes burdensome for a number of reasons. Maybe we lose sight of the reason for giving—God's "inexpressible gift"—and so our giving does not spring from gratitude. Or perhaps we fail to be realistic about our budgets. We forget that the things we buy can at best be mere tokens of oursleves, and so we grudgingly and anxiously overspend. Sometimes, too, we let our gift lists grow long without pruning, lacking the courage to say to extended family or friends, "Look, let's just exchange cards this year." We operate under time and budget pressures that kill the joy we should be feeling.

All of these are problems that can be dealt with so that Christmas giving, of all the ritual giving in the year, can become free and joyful, merry-hearted and untrammeled.

Realizing that the best gift is always the gift of ourselves, we should plan Christmas celebrations to include joy-filled times of preparation together. Baking together, decorating the house, planning and serving meals—all are happy activities and shared ones. Realizing that what the gift betokens is more important than the thing itself, we can select gifts sensitively and lovingly even within a carefully trimmed budget. Knowing that all joys are best shared, we can teach our families the joy of giving beyond the ritual circle by sharing our Christmas day with guests who do not have families of their own, or perhaps with people from another culture. Their questions and insights will enrich our own experience of Christmas.

"God loved; He gave." This is the story of Christmas, the

story on which the gospel message is built. In the ritual of giving and receiving in our culture, we have the joy of moving beyond mere thing-giving to real self-giving, and thus to make the gifts we choose show something more than just a social duty. It will become a little token of grace.

The Ritual of Receiving

Just as ritual giving can be moved by grace to something far more than social obligation, so ritual receiving and acknowledging can be touched by love and made into a return touch of grace. The other side of the ritualized gift is the formal acknowledgment. There are certainly "right ways" by which formal gifts are acknowledged. But truly gracious receiving will move beyond the form and recognize that a real thank you is far more than the gift given. A real thank you recognizes the giver as of greater value than the gift. A thank you that really warms the heart of the giver recognizes the gift as merely a token of a person and of that person's love and caring.

Because Cam and I teach in a small high school where the graduating class is never very large, we have been able to develop, over the years, a ritual of giving each graduate a small gift—something which serves as a token of our love for the student and our interest in his ongoing development—personal, intellectual, and spiritual. Each year we receive many kinds of thank you's: verbal thanks, simple and sincere; cards with little notes, each one special. And then, once in a while, we get a note that says something more: "Thank you for the gift. It reminded me just how much you both have meant to me. I will always remember you not just as teachers, but as special friends." It's that kind of note that tells the giver that he has not been obscured by the gift.

The secret of gracious receiving is to remember that the best thanks are always rendered by a person to a person: the personal note will always mean more than the formal card, however proper. What is special about the giver? What is special about the gift? If the acknowledgment simply and sincerely answers those two questions, it will affirm to the giver that time spent in careful choice or creation of the gift was indeed an investment.

Beyond Ritual Giving

While ritual giving and receiving are indeed important, and no one ignores with impunity the social codes which govern them, they surely should not represent the whole or even the greatest part of our giving. For Christian giving, springing from gratitude as it does, must find more than merely conventional outlets. It must find channels that direct giving to where it is most needed in a spontaneous and loving response. And it is to such spontaneous giving that we now turn our attention.

13

Giving As Response

When I am teaching, I usually stop to pick up my mail before school. One morning I found a strange, triangular package in the mailbox with the postmark "Tuktoyaktuk." It had been mailed in one of the most northerly settlements in Canada. I opened it, wondering who I knew up there and why I would be getting such a parcel.

Up from the wrapping stared a little arctic owl. The note read, "I hope you will accept this gift. It was carved from antelope horn by my uncle."

Accept it? Why, of course. With great joy.

It was sent by a young man whom I had never met, but with whom I had corresponded after sharing a hospital room with his mother. He wrote, "Sometimes when I can't make up my mind who I would like to write a letter to, I look in the family photos, and I saw your photo and the get-well card that you sent to my stepmother. She can't write as well as I can because I think she didn't go to school, so I thought I'd write and thank you." He asked me about the south

129

(that's where we live—at 53 degrees north latitude!), and I wrote to tell him about our lifestyle. A few more letters were exchanged, and then came the gift. That tiny arctic owl, smoothly shaped and shaded with the natural coloration of the horn from which it was carved, has brooded solemnly from a high shelf in our living room ever since.

It was another kind of gift altogether from the ritual giving discussed in the last chapter. It was a spontaneous gift, a response to friendship, a reaching out with one hand to receive our friendship; with the other to give a spontaneous, joyful gift.

Such giving is very much a part of living. It is the kind of giving and receiving involved in every family meal that is prepared and shared together. It celebrates that we do not live alone. Whether we send our mail from Tuktoyaktuk or New York City, we reach out to each other for fellowship, for a sense of community. And in that reaching out, in giving and receiving, we respond to each other and to life itself.

Giving as Response to a Person

Much of the glad giving in friendship, in family relationships, in Christian fellowship, is giving as response to other persons. The response of love is what prompts me to share a book of Luci Shaw's poems with a fellow-writer. It's not that I think my friend needs yet another book, for her home is almost as book-crammed as mine. It is just that I love her, appreciate her sensitivity to words, and want to celebrate this by sharing a special book with her. Or when I pour Cam yet another cup of tea after supper, it's not because I think he needs more tea; it's just that I want to share conversation with him a little longer.

It is this love-response to another person that is the essence of much spontaneous giving. The pleasure of the loved one is its goal. Anyone who has lived with little children knows the joy of sudden bouquets and fervently drawn pictures that are presented without ceremony as love-tokens. There need be no occasion. There is just the glad celebration of each other.

If you were to ask a child why, his answer might well be a little offended: "Because I love you." That's all. And that is surely the only excuse needed for spontaneous giving.

Of course, the ultimate love-response to a person is worship. We know so little about worship. And we know little of it in a spiritual sense because in our individualistic, self-centered society we know very little about its base: the giving to others of honor and respect. Writing to the Romans, Paul says, "Give everyone what you owe him: If you owe taxes, pay taxes; if revenue, then revenue; if respect, then respect; if honor, then honor. Let debt remain outstanding, except the continuing debt to love one another" (Romans 13:7,8). In a day when young people ape their elders in speaking disrespectfully of authorities, why should we be surprised that we know little of worship—that response of love and honor raised to its highest degree?

I realize, of course, that the matter could well be argued another way: perhaps we know little of how to give honor to each other because we know little of how to give worship to God. Whichever way it flows, the result is impoverishment of response. We fail to respond to God in a way showing our awareness of His worthiness; we fail to respond to each other in ways reflecting the ascription of worth.

This continuum from respect to honor to worship is clearly seen in the Anglican 1662 Book of Common Prayer of the Church of England, where the marriage ceremony includes an amazing line. The groom is to say to the bride, at the presentation of the ring, "With this ring I thee wed, with my body I thee worship...."

Since the changing value of words in the English language has made "worship" a much stronger and more exclusive word today than it was in 1662, more-recent versions of the Prayer Book have modified that amazing statement to, "With my body I thee honour...."

Whether in the older form or in the updated version, this startling little phrase puts the whole giving and receiving of sexual communion in an entirely different frame of reference from that with which we are familiar. How high this lifts it above mere animal copulation! In what high and holy esteem it holds the woman's body—so often exploited and demeaned in our society! In that single phrase, the mutual giving and receiving which constitutes truly human sexuality is given an unusual context. Sex becomes an act of adoration, of honor, of expression of highest esteem.

It all makes me think of my mother's definition of love, shared with us as teenagers: "Love is really the deepest form of respect one person can have for another."

If glad giving and joyful receiving is the natural response within a human love relationship—from friendship to marriage—how much more so should it naturally characterize our response to God as we come to know Him. A person who finds giving nothing but a burden is a person with very little sense of the goodness of God or of God's creation. When once we have really seen God as deserving of honor and as fully meriting our praise, when once the "wideness in His mercy" has awed us, when once His love has overwhelmed us, then giving is a glad response.

It makes perfect sense that the giving of our offerings should be part of our weekly gatherings for worship.[1] Unfortunately, in nonliturgical churches the worship of offering has often been obscured by lumping the act of giving together with other business items: "Announcements and Offering" is the slot on the bulletin. And so we fail, again and again, to touch on the glory that could be ours. We fail to see that, even as we receive from God through the reading of the Word and its declaration, so we gladly respond with our gifts of love—not out of any sense of grudging necessity, but in the same delighted joy which a bride and bridegroom share. "With our material goods, as with our lives and the expression of our lips, we Thee worship." Returning in dollars and cents a portion of what has been so graciously given to us may well be the duty of love—but it is a glad duty when once we have truly seen the Beloved. The raptures of the Songs of Solomon speak of self-giving in a way that the church has long understood at both the marital and devotional level.

In our small community we are part of a fellowship of believers where the church givings meet the immediate needs and reach out for mission. This year, when the treasurer balanced the books, she phoned me in great excitement. "Would you believe it?" she said; "Our offerings have tripled in the past four years." And yet this is a church which a few years earlier faced extinction because of financial problems. What changed it all? The love-response of individual people to God as His Word was declared and taught.

People give because their needs are met; they give in gratitude for a God who has made Himself real in a personal way to them; they give in glad worship. And Sunday after Sunday, as we rise to sing the ushers up the aisle with the "Old Hundredth," we worship together as an expression of worship—to the Lord. The church merely acts as God's distributor of that which is given in worship and love.

Response to a Need

The lane that led to our farmhouse was long, back in the days when I was at home with preschoolers. And I had felt isolated when we lived in town! Now, as Alberta winter winds piled drifts in the fields and packed long, solid bars of snow across that lane, I "stayed put" for days at a time. One winter Cam had a teaching job at a college located 35 miles away from the farm. His daily trip took him in the opposite direction from the village where we had to go to get our mail. So I was stranded at the end of a blown-in lane in a tiny house exploding with children. Most of the time I didn't mind being closed in with them. But what was really difficult for me was that often I was able to pick up my mail only once a week. And for me that constituted real hardship.

One Sunday morning at church I mentioned to some friends how long I was finding the weeks without mail. "I can stand almost anything except not hearing from outside,"

I confided. I didn't tell them that I wasn't even sure if there were an "outside" any longer.

"Well, I could help you with that," one of the women in the circle of our conversation said. "That is, if you would trust me with your mail-key." Edith drove a school bus morning and evening, and her plan was simple: "I'll pick up your mail every morning when I get mine, and then—if Cam will put up some kind of a receptacle—I will drop it off when I drive by on my way home."

Trust her with my mail-key? I would trust such a friend with my life! What a wonderful gift to a housebound mother—especially one who was just beginning to write, and for whom mail was the only way that any signals were coming through. Cam made a neat little mailbox and spray-painted it in two vivid shades of orange.

For the rest of that long winter, Edith would stop on her way home with her big yellow bus, long enough to tuck my mail into the bright orange mailbox. And each day, just before supper, I would slip out of the house and walk down that long lane to calm my heart and claim my mail. I think that Edith gave me far more than she ever guessed that winter. Sometimes I think that she gave me the gift of sanity.

Edith's giving was very different from the kind of ritual giving we were discussing in the last chapter. It was different, too, from giving in response to a person, although I count her a dear friend. Hers was giving in response to an observed need.

Learning to See

Of course, in order to become response givers we must first learn to see needs. Learning to see with our hearts is important. In an age of media presentation of thousands of emotional appeals in the course of a year, we have to learn how to *really* see, to *really* feel, all over again. There is the constant danger of anesthetizing ourselves, of numbing ourselves, if only as a defense against the overwhelming needs to which we are continuously exposed and which we so often feel helpless to correct.

But this was never Jesus' way. And it cannot be ours.

First, we must really want to see needs. This is part of what Jesus showed in the story of the Good Samaritan. The priest did not want to see the needs of the hurting man. To see was to be forced to respond. And so the priest solved the whole matter very neatly: he crossed to the other side of the road to avoid having to see the need of the man who lay wounded on the path.

If we want to begin to give responsively, we will have to begin by praying, "Lord, open my eyes. Let me see this world through Your eyes, seeing needs as You do. And then open my heart and my hands, and show me how to respond."

I remember a young pastor telling how, prior to entering the ministry, he prayed a prayer like this: "Oh Lord, give me a heart tender to the needs of people around me. Give me Your love for the people I meet." In only a few days, finding himself breaking into tears as he walked down a street or sat in a bus depot, unable to bear the heartache that God had shared with him, the young man had to pray again, "Lord, take away this burden of compassion. I can't handle Your love. Give me just as much love as I can hold and use."

Of course, not all need-responding has to be at that deeply exhausting a level. It can be as practical as my mother-in-law bringing me a new potato-peeler of the kind she had used for years, simply because she had seen me struggling with the conventional type. "They never worked for me," she observed. "Here, try this." That little spontaneous gift, remembered often when I am hurrying to prepare a big pot of potatoes, revolutionized my potato-peeling!

Learning to Respond

Of course, it is not enough to merely *see* needs; the whole purpose of seeing is that we might *respond*. The disciples saw a lot of tired, hungry people at the end of a teaching day. They saw the need. But their response was, "Send the crowds away." Jesus, seeing trhe same needs, "had compassion." He saw them as sheep without a shepherd. And He instructed His disciples, "You give them something to eat" (Matthew 14:14-16).

Giving in resonse to need takes little more than a loving, sensitive heart and the personal strength to overcome the inertia of selfishness—and to reach out. With the little we have in our hands, backed up by our Lord's resources, the needs that we feel are beyond us can be met. And surely many little, homely needs—from buttons on shirts to time to talk—can be met by people whose eyes and hands are well coordinated.

As we begin to pray, "Lord, help me to see the needs as You see them," we will begin to see people and their problems in a different perspective. Needs that we thought were pressing may not be as important as other needs that we are prone to ignore. A person's loneliness may be a far greater need than his health, even though we would normally be concerned first about health and then about other needs.

I find an aerial photo of our farm to be a fascinating thing. Things that seem very important from my ground-view (the peeling paint on a window frame, the garden needing attention) have no importance at all from the air. Now the buildings become little dollhouses, or, from higher up, tiny cubes. But other, bigger problems—not obvious from the ground—take on a new significance in the study of an aerial photograph. The way in which water runoff is eroding a nearby field, pushing fingers deeper and deeper into the land, takes on its proper seriousnesss.

And so it is in the spiritual perception of human need. All too often we sense physical and emotional needs, and attempt to meet these, when they are actually only symptomatic of the deeper needs of the spirit. We need to be Spirit-taught, to learn God's pattern of priorities. The best pattern for our caring for others will be that set by our Lord, who "went around doing good" (Acts 10:38).

At their best, Christian missions have represented this kind of concern for whole persons and whole societies. At less than their best, we have erred on the right hand by failing to see the wholeness of people, by failing to understand the implications of the gospel for every area of human interaction, including the economic and the political. Or we have erred on the left hand by failing to see that even if we have done everything possible for the improvement of people's physical condition, we have still given them nothing if we have failed to introduce them to Jesus Christ as living Lord.

How Much Is Enough?

As we begin to see needs, we will also have to learn in what ways we can respond. The danger of under-response is always with us. We are tied up with ourselves, tied up with building our own little kingdoms. We find it hard to give priority to the kingdom of God, where people and their needs have a place well above things. Responding requires acknowledgment that other people have claims on our resources—claims which may be even more legitimate than our own. Responding requires us to recognize that God's claim on our resources—and indeed on ourselves—is absolute.

If under-response is one danger, another is that we might have a purely intellectual response to human need, like the Levite in Jesus' story of the Good Samaritan. We may take note of the need and really feel something about it, but we have deadlines, schedules, religious busyness to be about—and we just can't stop. Feeling pity is not an adequate response to a perceived need; something must actually be done. The Samaritan felt the pity and had the intellectual response—and then he acted, demonstrating that compassion must be translated into action to be of any value.

The third danger in response is that of over-response. It may be impossible to meet every need of which we are aware, especially if we become truly sensitive to need.

I remember how, at our wedding reception, a vibrant young soloist sang (at our request) "Let Them Burn Out for Thee." It was indeed the desire of our hearts. And we almost did—several times. In fact, it took a good many years of living at the brink of health breakdown before I learned to pray differently.

Jesus Himself took measure to avoid crowds, crowds where He knew He would be confronted with need. And He pointedly withdrew His disciples. My sisters and I used to be visited with uncontrollable giggles when we read Jesus' invitation (in the King James Version) to "come ye apart." I have since learned that if we fail to come apart in response to our Master, we may well come apart physically and emotionally.

How are we to go about balancing our lives to reflect both our awareness of need and our response to it? Having prayed that God would show us the true needs of those around us, we need to carry our prayer further, asking Him to underline in our hearts the needs He wills for us to meet. Ultimately, even giving that responds to need must first be giving in response to *Him*.

I got a glimpse of the importance of this when a seatmate bragged to me about all the good that his service club was involved in "Yeah," he said, "we have a big program for crippled kids. Getting them to camp and stuff, you know."

"That must really make you feel great," I commented.

He shrugged. "Not particularly. But somebody has to do it."

Again I realized how different Christian giving is from all other giving, for that which arises in glad gratitude to a Person find its channels in response to other persons and their needs. And joy is its return.

14

Love Knows No Difference

The school year was almost over. Wearily I picked up my last pile of test papers. I almost hated to look at them, silent witnesses to just how little I had been able to give my students, especially this class. I sighed. First-year high school students, these students were "language arts deficient." And that was putting it nicely!

Mechanically I scanned the first questions, striking through incorrect answers with my red pencil. As a sample short story for them to read and respond to it, I had included the story of the Prodigal Son from Luke 15. The questions, to be answered in complete sentences, were simple and straightforward: "Who are the main characters in this story?" "Where in the story does the climax occur?" The last question was designed to test both their understanding of the story and their ability to derive meaning from context: "In the context of this story, what does the word 'prodigal' mean?" I had thought that question was clear and straightforward. But as I began to read through the answers, laying paper after paper on the pile, I discovered that the meaning of the term "prodigal" was by no means self-evident. There were wild guesses and gaping blanks.

And then I picked up Ted's paper. He was an earnest student. I wished him well as, red pencil poised above his answer, I began to read. "From this story," his angular, penciled answer said, "I get that prodigal means happy and forgiven."

A cry of joy formed—although I didn't quite utter it. Wonderful, oh wonderful! I, who had wanted to be the gift-giver to these students, had just been given a most incredible gift: a contextual definition of a word I had long taken for granted, a definition which had theological implications far beyond what my student could have dreamed.

For Ted's answer had shown me something that went far beyond denotation. In the context of the gospel, "prodigal" or "sinner" takes on an entirely new meaning: the waster becomes the beloved son, happy and forgiven.

Teacher / Learner

And so it has often been that at the moment when I have thought it most important that I give, I have become the receiver. I read an article recently by friend and colleague, David Watts, in which he characterizes himself as "a sometime artist, a longtime student, and a teacher/learner with young children over the past six years."[1] Oh, yes, I find myself responding: a teacher/learner. Love refuses to recognize the distinction.

The very richest teaching experiences are those in which the teacher becomes a learner with and from his students. In an atmosphere of shared exploration, teacher/learner and learner/teacher becomes a living unity, a community of learning. Idealistic? Of course. As a teacher, however, I have had enough of those magic times with students to know that it is an ideal which can sometimes be realized...but only when we become aware that our students need not only to learn, but also to teach.

Parent / Child

It is so in our family living, too. We characterize the parental posture as a giving one and the childhood posture as a receiving one. And yet, as we live it out, we find ourselves gifted by our children in many wonderful, unexpected ways.

When the children were smaller, I found myself a player in a little ritual drama as each Mother's Day approached.

"What do you want for Mother's Day, Mom?"

"Oh—a hug and a kiss. And a good girl...."

An impatient little face would say, "Oh, Mom. What do you *really* want?"

And on Mother's Day, I would find a pile of homemade gifts beside my breakfast plate, each wrapped with more Scotch-tape than I would use in a whole Christmas season. There were stories, poems, drawings, bookmarks—each item lovingly prepared.

But such little gifts are only the shadows of the real gifts my children have continually given me. For they have enriched me with an insight into the loving heart of God, a new understanding of my own relationship with Him, and a fresh sense of wonder as I walk in His world.

I remember the moment our eldest was born—a son, whole and healthy. Gratitude swept over me, and then a wave of intense love. How I loved that tiny purple baby. In one overwhelming moment I felt compassion, fierce protectiveness, and indescribable tenderness.

Later, I would ask myself—"Why? Why did I love that tiny baby so? Where did such love come from?" And I would understand that God the Father had given me a tiny heartbeat—just a pulse of His love. Undeserved, unearned love came to our child for no reason except that he had been born to us. And suddenly, I had a whole new understanding of God's love for us as His children.

And thus, in becoming a parent, I came to a deepening of my understanding of what it meant to be a child: God's child. In becoming His children through faith in the Lord

Jesus Christ (see John 1:12) we are immersed in an ocean of unmerited, undeserved love...love that doesn't depend on what we *do*, but is given to us freely because of who we are.

That is grace. And mother-love, extended to a baby in his weakness, in his inability to do anything but *be*, taught me just a little more about it. That knowledge is a gift my children gave me, each one, just by being born.

They have given me another great gift: a new understanding of the trusting, love relationship into which we are invited at the moment we truly say, "Our Father...." Nothing melts a parent's heart more than the physical attitude of trust: the tiny fingers that curve around yours, clinging trustingly like tendrils; the little rosebud mouth, sucking reflexively, seeking the breast. Later, the smooth, chubby arm that wraps around your neck in a reassuring—if nearly choking—hug. Or the hand that reaches for yours as you watch an electrical storm together.

Every physical posture of trust expresses an underlying attitude of trust: "Life is good. I am loved. All is well." In enjoying their trust, I have learned more of the quiet, trusting relationship God desires with His children.

I have also learned from my children a little more of the meaning of, "according to your faith, be it unto you." I remember a bedtime talk with one of the boys. Christmas was coming, and our son confidently anticipated it. "You know, Mom, I think Daddy will get me an electric train," he said.

"Oh?" I asked, amused by his certainty. "What makes you think so?"

"Well," the six-year-old reasoned, "when I wanted a wagon, he got me one for my birthday. And when I was ready to ride a bike, he got one for me. So I think now that I'm old enough to have an electric train, he'll get it for me. You know something? Dad seems to get a kick out of getting me what I really want."

I went away from his bedside, blessed. On the basis of God's past unchanging goodness and His loving fatherhood, I could ask in joyful anticipation of receiving "the desires of [my] heart." (Psalm 37:5).

Not only have I had new insights into the loving heart of God and nature of the trust-relationship into which He invites me; through the eyes and words of my children I have also been given a fresh outlook on the created world, an outlook in which every day is touched with wonder. When the children were small, there were fresh metaphors and wonderful new discoveries daily. And the sense of wonder has grown with them. One day one comes home from school commenting on the amazing mechanism of the body's immune system; another day, a new author is added to our list of "let's read everything by this one." Or, as we drive to school, a teenager comments, "I think a foal is such a perfect thing—life stripped down to its essence; all bone and muscle, with nothing left over." And every new colt I see becomes a parable.

Standing with a child out under the brilliant spread of the northern lights one August midnight, I suddenly saw, with him, that the pattern of the light was of a great wing spread across the sky, every feather painted in white-green light. And suddenly, "Under his wings / I am safely abiding," had a new visual context for me.

The children's sense of wonder has extended beyond that created world. They have brought that same freshness to our reading of God's Word. I will never forget the time I read them the Sermon on the Mount from a contemporary translation. "I say, 'Love your enemies!' Pray for those who persecute you" (Matthew 5:43,44).

Geoffrey and Cammie-Lou, then about 10 and 8 years old, broke into incredulous laughter. "He's got to be kidding!" Geoff said. "How can anyone love his enemies?"

And suddenly, those old, familiar words broke through on me with something of their intended force. How radical

Jesus' teaching really is—and how impossible to obey apart from the regenerating and infilling of the Holy Spirit.

Giver / Receiver

Of course, in relationships of full mutuality—in marriage, in friendship—the reciprocation of giving and receiving is even more obvious. One cannot give joy without receiving it. Love gives in receiving, receives in giving, and keeps no account book.

In my spiritual life, too, the process of learning how to both give and receive goes on. It began—this strange, stumbling pilgrimage toward discipleship—with an open "Yes" to the grace of God as revealed in Jesus Christ. A receiving. Or was it a giving? For in receiving the life of Christ, I have given Him mine. It was an exchange of lives: my little mortal one for His great eternal one.

Later I would discover the principle, deep in the heart of the Christian experience, of relinquishment. Relinquishment is the cross that accompanies the call to discipleship. The further one presses on to know Christ, the more clear it becomes that only what has been truly given to God can be received back from Him, transformed by His touch into something whole and serviceable in His kingdom.

Again and again I am called to toil up Mount Moriah, beside gnarled old Abraham, to offer up to God some darling of my heart.

One of those trips took place on a dark night in a hospital when I felt I was dying. "You don't want to take me home yet, Lord," I found myself arguing. "I have only begun to write for You." A copy of my first book shiny and new, lay on the windowsill close to my bed. "Surely You want me to do more."

And then the Lord showed me: "All that you do on this side will only look like scribblings in a copybook when you get to the other side. You're just practicing now for an eternity of praising me. Are you willing to let your writing go?"

At last I could say, "Yes, Lord. If this is all You want me to do on this side, I can lay it down now."

And then, of course, I argued with Him on the basis of my family. "Lord, You don't want to call me yet, because Cam and the children need me." On top of the copy of my first book, a gold frame enclosed the picture of all that was dearest to me. The children were still small, a covey of little ones. How could He ask me to leave them?

And again He spoke: "Are they yours—or are they mine?"

I wrestled with that question through the flame of pain and the fog of drugs until at last I could say, clearly and decisively, "They are Yours, Lord. They always have been. I give them over to Your care, and I trust You to bring them home to Yourself safely."

At last, I was ready to respond. "If You are calling me now, Lord Jesus, I'll come," I whispered at last. It was a final relinquishment of that which I loved—life itself.

Then He met me in a glow of golden light that seemed to emanate from near the foot of my bed, and my heart leaped up with joy and love. I knew that it was He whom I loved most, that it was He who loved me best.

A peace flooded over me, a surging ocean of love for my Saviour, into whose outstretched hands I had committed all that I loved. It was as though He spoke to me the ancient words: "Do not be afraid...I am your shield, your very great reward" (Genesis 15:1).

In a few moments the glory faded from my vision, but never from my spirit. I didn't die that night. Not physically. But I had walked that lonely mountain trail and had relinquished to God my life, my family, and my work—all that I had. And as He released me back to all three, I felt the glory of resurrection life. I was living, quite literally, on the other side of death.

The act of relinquishment is giving at its most intense, its most painful. It is the kind of giving that must be done by sharing with faithful Abraham the confidence "that God could raise the dead," remembering that "figuratively speaking, he did receive Isaac back from death" (Hebrews 11:19).

There is the painful moment of release, of giving over—and then the glad, unspeakable joy of receiving, in resurrection glory, the Lord Jesus Himself. And then the dream, the person, the goal that hurt so much to let go—the very thing that has been relinquished—is often gloriously restored to your hand.

Transformed, it is no longer a thing to be served, but now a means of serving the one true God. But it no longer really matters whether He takes it forever or hands it back, for now it is His. In its place stands Jesus Christ, Lord of all. And even the most reluctant, pain-ridden giver acknowledges that in Christ he has received beyond all his imaginings.

As the beggared prodigal son had to allow himself to be stripped in order to be garbed in the robe of sonship, so we must relinquish whatever we clutch most closely—our demands on life, our claims on our children, our bargains with God—in order to receive, open-handed and empty-handed, the gifts He wants to give us.

With each relinquishment, we learn something more of the gift of God's grace to us. He does not ask from us the darlings of our heart because He desires to hurt us or to rob us—never! He asks of us only that we may learn more of what it is to be the children of God, re-made in His image.

In our moments of painful relinquishment, of "giving over," we come to understand more of His awesome self-giving. "For God so loved the world, that He gave..." (John 3:16). And that Son whom He gave relinquished every claim, finally uttering the ultimate prayer, "Not my will, but Yours be done" (Luke 22:42) in order to accomplish our salvation.

And so, as we give and as we receive, we find our lives more deeply buried in His heart of love. It is the heart of the Giver. It is there, and only there, that we learn the love which finally removes all distinction between giving and receiving. Awed by grace, made whole by such love, we can begin to really live. Because we are receivers, we can truly, freely give.

Notes

Introduction

1. Luci Shaw, "Gifts for My Girl," in *The Sighting* (Wheaton: Harold Shaw, 1981), pp. 38-40.

Chapter 1

1. See James 5:14-16. I believe that the correct order of things is to seek prayer by the elders of your church. This is possible only if you are in a church where the

elders practice healing prayer in accordance with the Scriptures. Since we were not in such a church situation at that time, the Lord directed me to have Lucetta pray for me.

Chapter 2

1. C.S. Lewis, *Screwtape Letters* (London: Collins [Fontana], 1955), pp. 108-10.
2. Carol Ryrie Brink, *Lad With a Whistle* (New York: Macmillan, 1947), p. 208.
3. Aleksandr I. Solzhenitsyn, *The Gulag Archipelago, I-II* (New York: Harper & Row, 1979), pp. 54-56.
4. A.W. Tozer, *The Pursuit of God* (Harrisburg: Christian Publications, 1958), p. 23.

Chapter 3

1. Sinclair Lewis, *Main Street* (New York: Harcourt, Brace and Company, 1920), p. 69.
2. I. B. Sergei, "My God and I," in *Country and Western Hymnal* (Grand Rapids: Singspiration Music, 1972).
3. Annie Dillard, *Holy the Firm* (New York: Harper & Row, 1977), p. 59.
4. Robertson Davies, *A Mixture of Frailties* (Toronto: Macmillan, 1958), p. 78.

Chapter 4

1. John Donne, "The Indifferent," in *John Donne: Poetry and Prose* (Oxford: Clarendon Press, 1946), p. 14.
2. William Shakespeare, *Richard III*, V:iii:120.

Chapter 5

1. Copyright Steven Barrie & Co., Inc., Southampton, PA, 1977.
2. *Richard Scarry's Best Rainy Day Book Ever* (New York: Random House, 1974).

Chapter 6

1. Henri J. M. Nouwen, *Making All Things New* (New York: Harper & Row, 1981), p. 70.

Chapter 10

1. Hans Seyle, *Stress Without Distress* (New York: New American Library [Signet], 1975), pp. 122-31.

Chapter 13

1. For a fuller development of my ideas on giving to the Lord, you might like to look at Chapter 6, "Basic Needs I: Sharing the Good Things," in my earlier book, *Living on Less and Liking It More* (Chicago: Moody Press, 1976), pp. 70-85.

Chapter 14

1. David W. Watts, "Creativity and Catharsis," in *The ATA Magazine*, Dec. 1982, p. 17.

OTHER BOOKS
BY MAXINE HANCOCK

Love, Honor and Be Free
Living on Less and Liking It More
Confident, Creative Children
The Forever Principle